MOTO
BOATING
BASICS

The step-by-step guide to owning, helming and maintaining a motor boat

Jon Mendez

ADLARD COLES

LONDON • OXFORD • NEW YORK • NEW DELHI • SYDNEY

Contents

BOAT HANDLING
how to

BERTHING
how to

Introduction

I was lucky enough to grow up in a boating family, absorbing most of my knowledge through osmosis rather than from a book or in a classroom. But it was only when I started reading, and ultimately working for, *Motor Boat & Yachting* magazine that I realised how much I didn't know. For someone who'd already owned a boat for more than ten years, it was quite an eye-opener and a salutary lesson in the danger of overestimating your own ability. So how much more daunting must it be for someone new to boating to take that first step towards buying or chartering a boat?

I decided there and then to commission a series of monthly articles that would help readers of all different experience levels master the essentials of owning, driving and maintaining a boat. To ensure they would all be as clear and easy to understand as possible, each of these skills would be broken down into six simple steps with photographs, explanations and accompanying videos showing you exactly how it should be done. Many thanks to Richard Langdon for the excellent photos and videos.

When it came to selecting the best possible author/presenter for the task, one name instantly sprang to mind. Jon Mendez isn't just one of the most experienced boat skippers around, having taught and examined hundreds of RYA instructors over the years as well as delivering boats all over the world, he also has an uncanny ability to explain complex things in easy-to-understand language.

So popular has the resulting series become, running for over four years and clocking up more than a million views on YouTube, that it seemed only sensible to package them all together into a single comprehensive book. *Motor Boating Basics* is the culmination of that project; a single, easy-to-follow publication that covers all the key skills needed to run your own motor boat.

From learning how to manoeuvre a single-engined craft into a tight berth to retrieving a man overboard, changing a fuel filter or simply coiling a rope, it teaches you the techniques to get it right first time, every time. Even if you think you know how to do it correctly, I guarantee you will pick up some valuable new tip or word of advice from Jon's years of experience that will make it that bit quicker and easier.

To help you navigate your way around the book, we have broken these skills down into five sections covering essential skills, boat maintenance, navigation, boat handling and berthing. I make no excuses for the latter section also being the joint-largest one. Nothing causes as much anxiety among boat owners as berthing their boat, especially if strong winds, limited manoeuvring space or even an engine failure makes this more challenging than usual. We have tried to cover all these eventualities and more, including the art of coming alongside single-handed.

I have been following Jon's step-by-step guides for years now and have become a much more confident and competent skipper as a result. I am certain that by reading this book, you will too. Above all, enjoy the learning process, practise your new skills whenever the opportunity allows and take pride in becoming a better skipper. The more relaxed you are, the more fun you and your guests will have.

Happy boating!

Hugo Andreae

Hugo Andreae
Editor – *Motor Boat & Yachting*

To watch the videos showing each skill in this book in action, go to mby.com/howto.

essential skills

how to

how to
USE THE RIGHT KNOT

Unlike our sailing cousins, as a motor boater we don't need to know dozens of different knots. However, there are four essential knots that you really do need to know how to tie and when to use: a bowline, a clove hitch, a round turn and two half hitches, and a sheet bend.

All four need practice and regular use to ensure tying them becomes second nature, as like every skill, the ability to do so fades with time and lack of use.

Bowline

The traditional Boy Scout knot, its greatest asset is that once tied and pulled tight, it creates a secure loop that can be passed through cleats or tied around items such as riser rails or rings. As long as there's tension on the line, it will remain secure. I use it regularly to pass through the centre of cleats and then loop up and over the ears to give a really secure and almost chafe-free attachment. However, you do need to be careful as its greatest asset (its security under tension) is also its greatest issue as you cannot untie it with any load on the line, so never use it unless you can free the other end of the line to release the tension.

Clove hitch

A very simple knot, this allows you to quickly fasten a line around something, such as a guard wire or rail. It's great for tying on fenders and is easy to adjust simply by releasing some tension on the crossover and shortening or lengthening the lines. The danger is that if that tension comes off the line, for example when the fenders touch the water, then it can self -release. To make it more secure you can make extra turns before passing the line through itself or pass a half hitch over the end with the load on to stop it loosening.

Round turn and two half hitches

This is perhaps the knot I like best, because it's so versatile and easy to tie. You can pass a whole turn around whatever you want – cleat centres, handrails, rings or posts – and then finish it off with a pair of half hitches, both tied in the same direction. It's compact, has very little chafe, and best of all it's very secure but can be undone even with a load on it – for example on a falling tide. This also needs watching as the unwary can undo something, not realising that it may be under considerable tension. It's also great for fenders that are not going to be adjusted for a while and must not slip.

Sheet bend

A simple but often forgotten knot, this is very handy for tying two ropes together. I find it invaluable for things like rafting up when you need long shorelines but all yours are too short. It looks the same as a bowline but is composed of two different ropes. If the ropes are of different thickness then it's usual to tie the thinner one to the thicker. It's also superb for tow lines, but be warned, if you have applied a lot of weight, the knot may require some serious persuasion to undo.

1 Bowline Ideal for making loops in dock lines. Twist the standing line clockwise over itself to create a small loop, making sure that the loose end crosses over the standing part (not under it), then pass the tail end up through the back of the loop, round the back of the standing line and back down through the loop before pulling it tight.

2 Bowline on a cleat Once you have tightened the bowline to secure it, you can pass the main loop that you've created through the centre of an open cleat and hook it back over the horns. This is very secure and avoids the possibility of chafing the rope.

3 Clove hitch Great for fenders. Pass the line over the railing and back under, then cross it over the standing line as you pass it back over the railing. Leave the crossing part loose, tuck the tail end under it and tighten.

4 Round turn and two half hitches Pass the line over the railing twice, then pass the loose end around the standing line and tuck it through the top of the loop to create the first half hitch, and repeat for the second.

5 Sheet bend
Used for joining two ropes together. Create a loop in the thicker of the two lines (in this case the black and red one) then pass the thinner white line up through the back of the loop, around the back of it and then tuck the tail end under the standing part of the white line.

6 Sheet bend on a tow line This makes a secure towing bridle and as long as you have an open end on the red and black line it's easy to centre the tow behind by adjusting that end on your boat's aft cleat.

how to
LASSO A CLEAT

Lassoing a cleat or post with a line can be extremely useful when you're being pushed off a berth by the wind, or the skipper is having a hard time coming alongside. It works equally well on a line taken from a stern, mid-ship or bow cleat but we are showing a bow line as that's usually the hardest due to the height difference.

The first task is for the skipper to balance the boat on the elements to hold it stationary. The next is to brief the crew on the plan, place an extra fender closest to the point of contact and choose a suitable line. This needs to be long enough to reach from your chosen cleat, go around your selected target and travel back to the cleat leaving enough slack to be tied off safely, but not so long or heavy as to be unwieldy.

The perfect technique

Place one end on the cleat, pass the line under the rails, then coil it into equal-sized loops by holding the cleated end in one hand and using the other to draw out an arm's length of rope before looping it back into your fixed hand. Make two or three coils and then place a finger across them, before making two or three more coils. This splits them into two sets and ensures you pick up the latest set with your free hand once you've finished making them.

Hold the tail end in one hand with half the coils on top (if your hands aren't big enough, take the loose end back under the rail and stand on it) then put the other set of coils in your other hand. The key to throwing them is not to aim down at the target cleat but up and outwards. Bring your hands to your chest and throw your arms up and outwards. This creates a nice big loop that hopefully falls down over the cleat.

Now bring the loose end under the rails and gradually pull in the excess slack to leave a short but still slightly loose line – don't pull it in tight or it will snub the bow in too close and prevent the stern from coming alongside – then make it off on the cleat aboard. Personally, I am wary of holding lines with just a single turn around a cleat as I have seen too many trapped fingers happen – properly cleated off is safer but you need to judge the amount of slack required.

To use the lassoed line to help the rest of the boat into the berth, take up the slack by letting the elements push the bow out or by gently going in and out of gear on the outside engine until you feel the line come tight. As this happens, engage the outside engine astern and leave it in gear. This will pull the line taut and bring the stern of the boat towards the pontoon. By keeping pressure on the line, the boat will swing in under control. If you are concerned about the line pressure, a nudge ahead on the inside engine will ease the tension and assist the turn.

Just before the stern touches the pontoon, take the boat out of gear momentarily so it kisses the pontoon, then back into gear to hold it alongside whilst you attach further lines. The principles are the same when using a stern line, just be extra careful if you have a sharply angled bathing platform as they are hard to fender well.

1 Coiling the line

Take the line under the rails, then use one arm to hold the attached end of the line while the other measures out the next length of rope before looping back into the first hand.

2 Splitting the coils

The magic finger placed across the first three coils allows you to separate them from the next three. Now pick up the top three coils with your right hand, leaving the others in your left.

3 Throwing

Hold your hands together on your chest, then throw them up and outwards, releasing the coils. Do not look down at the cleat – look up at the arc of rope you want to see. It will naturally drop over the cleat.

4 Taking up the slack
Bring the loose line end back under the rail and remove most of the slack before cleating off. Then allow the boat to drop back and take up the tension using the elements or a nudge of astern on the outside engine if needed.

5 Bringing the stern in
Once the line has gone taut put the outside engine in astern to keep the tension on and pull the stern in. Keep the boat in gear and as the stern closes in on the pontoon, the bow will move away.

6 Coming alongside
Leave the engine in gear until the last second, then momentarily shift into neutral just before it touches, to soften the impact before going back into astern to hold the boat alongside while you attach a stern line.

how to
COIL MOORING LINES

Coiling and storing ropes can be one of the simplest but most frustrating tasks on a boat. There are few things more annoying than taking a rope out of its locker only to find it's a tangled, unusable mess.

There are a multitude of ways to coil a rope neatly and many boaters will already have a favoured method. However, for those who still struggle with it, here is my preferred way of doing it with a couple of alternative finishes depending on how you want to store it.

Different ropes require slightly different techniques. Traditional three-strand rope (like the white one in the images) is made with a clockwise twist to the line and when you coil it, it's easier to coil it in a clockwise manner with each coil following how the rope was made. This helps the rope sit naturally and extends its lifespan. More modern braid on braid ropes are not constructed in the same manner so you don't need to put a twist in each coil. However, it does still make the rope much neater and easier to stow and reuse.

Coiling

The first task with all rope is to run it through your hands and flake it on to the deck. This removes any twists or kinks and allows you to check that the rope hasn't picked up any debris or snags. A rope is generally divided into two parts: a bight, which is the slack part that you make by picking the rope up; and the standing part, which is generally the rest. So, having picked up the rope; lay one end into your open hand (usually the left hand if you're right-handed or vice versa) with the end facing whichever way will allow you to coil the rope in a clockwise direction. I now tuck the elbow of the hand holding the rope end against my body to give it support and slide my free hand a full arm's length along the rope, grasp it and bring it back across my body to my other hand. Just before I lay this

first coil on to the open hand, I twist it a 'half turn' in a clockwise direction. This has two purposes: first, to get the rope to coil in line with its construction, and second, to give nice flat coils that sit neatly and are easier to store. I keep repeating this until I have about 1.5m (4.9ft) of rope left. I then pass this remaining 1.5m (4.9ft) around the back of the coils, tucking the end under a finger to hold it whilst I bring the rest round the front of the coils. I then pass it around again but this time I cross it over the first turn to lock

the coils in place. I keep going like this for four or more turns so it's secure before deciding how I want to end it.

Endings

There are various different ways to end the coiling process, depending on whether you want to hang it up or place it in a locker. To hang, I just pull through an end with a long enough tail to tie it on to something. If it's going to be hung for a while, then you may need something more secure, so this time, pass a loop through your coils then pass the loose end through the loop, pull tight and hang up.

For stowing in a locker, I pass the loop through as before but this time bring that loop up over the top of the coils and pull it tight. This secures it really well for locker storage, but if hung up, it tends to leave a kink in the coils. Lastly, if the rope is too heavy or too long, coil it round a cleat or winch, or simply coil it on the deck.

1 Preparation
Before starting, run the rope through your hand and place it on the deck. This will free up any tangles and allow you to feel for any damage, debris or snags. The line on the left is three-strand and needs clockwise coiling. The other two are braided ropes.

2 First loop If
you're right-handed, lay the rope in your left hand with the end facing in towards your body, then slide your free arm along the rope to its full extension, grasp it and bring it back to create the first coil. As you do this, give the rope a half twist outwards before laying the coil in a clockwise manner.

3 Coiling Repeat
the process until you have completed your coils, then pass the line around the back of the coils. I like to hold the line with my little finger so it doesn't fall off while I bring the second locking turn around the front.

4 Ending 1 This is the ending I use for hanging the coiled line on a hook or rail. Just pass the loose end through the top of the coils, ensuring there is enough free line to secure it to a rail but not so much that it trails on to the deck or bilges. If the coil is placed in a locker, the lack of a locking turn means it can come loose.

5 Ending 2 This time, a loop is passed through the top of the coils and the loose end is taken through that loop and pulled tight. This locks the coils and is much more secure. It can be used either for hanging or placing in a locker.

6 Ending 3 The final technique is to pass through a loop as before, but this time take the loop up and over the top of the coils. It's very secure and great for lockers but does not hang nearly as well.

how to
TIE UP YOUR BOAT

A wander around any marina will reveal a hundred different variations of how to tie up a boat and to be fair, there is no universal one-size-fits-all answer. However, while many of the solutions on show are perfectly valid, there are also plenty of boat owners with very little understanding of what the lines are supposed to do and in some cases, it's a miracle the boat's still there when the owners return.

For an alongside berth in a non-tidal marina, or one with floating pontoons, you need a minimum of four lines. The bow line should lead forwards from the bow cleat to a cleat on the pontoon a short distance in front of it. The stern line should lead aft from a stern cleat to a pontoon cleat a little way behind it. These bow and stern lines are to keep the boat alongside. Then comes a pair of springs to stop the vessel surging fore and aft in the elements.

The correct terminology for spring lines always causes some debate. As far as I'm concerned, a line that stops the boat from moving backwards is a stern or aft spring and usually runs forwards from the boat's stern or mid cleat to a pontoon cleat several metres ahead of it. One that stops forward movement is a bow or fore spring and usually runs from a bow or mid cleat to a pontoon cleat several metres astern of it.

I always like the bow and stern lines to have a touch of slack in them so that the boat is 'relaxed' on its berth and can move a little way out from the pontoon rather than being pinned against it, rubbing on its fenders all the time. In contrast to this, I like the springs reasonably taut so that any fore and aft movement is kept to a minimum.

Most boats are tied up in this manner; it is usually how the lines are set up on a cleat, known as the lead, that is incorrect. This lead is very important as it ensures the correct loading of a cleat and minimises wear on both the rope and the boat. It also allows the load to be released

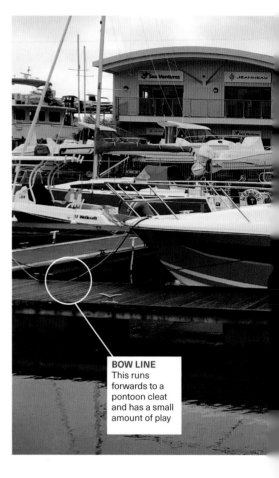

BOW LINE
This runs forwards to a pontoon cleat and has a small amount of play

easily when the time comes to leave. A lead can be described as 'open' or 'closed' – we always want an open lead as this covers all of the above conditions.

Unlike sailors, who usually like to use a different line for each job, motor boaters are usually more pragmatic and often use one longer line to do two jobs, such as the bow line and stern spring or stern line and bow spring. To tie a motor boat up with two long lines, lead the stern line aft and make it off on the pontoon cleat ashore using the '0880' technique (see step 4), then

AFT/STERN SPRING
This stops the boat moving backwards and should be taut

FORE/BOW SPRING
This stops the boat moving forwards and should be taut

STERN LINE
This runs aft to a pontoon cleat and has a small amount of play in it

return it by going forwards to a centre cleat aboard the boat – this makes it a spring. Since this line will be stopping any forward movement, it is called a bow or fore spring even though it runs from a cleat positioned astern of the boat.

Repeat the same process with the bow line, ie lead it forwards and make it off to a cleat ashore, then return it to a centre cleat on the vessel to act as a stern spring stopping any backward movement of the vessel. The disadvantage of using two long lines instead of four shorter ones is that any adjustments to the bow or stern line means undoing the springs first.

The other consideration is where to start. Either start the line on board with a bowline or made-up loop and then tidy up the loose ends on the pontoon, or start with the loops down on the pontoon cleats and leave the tails on the boat, which looks neater but means more hassle when leaving. This is one area where the motor-boat style of using two longer lines has an advantage as all the tails end up tidily back aboard. Leaving is also simple as the springs naturally have to come off first. The choice is yours; so long as they're led and made off correctly, the boat will be secure.

1 Incorrect lead
The way you lead the rope around the cleat is crucial to tying up a boat correctly. Here, the lead is the wrong way around the cleat and is described as 'closed'. The weight and wear are on the toe rail instead of the cleat, causing premature wear to the gelcoat and the rope. It also makes it difficult to tension the line by 'sweating' it in.

2 Correct lead
Now the wear and weight of the boat is on the cleat rather than the gelcoat. You or your crew can now assist with tensioning the line by keeping the line taut with your right hand while pulling on the standing part of the line and sweating in the slack.

3 Boat to shore
When running a stern line from the boat to the shore, it has to go from the boat's stern cleat to a pontoon cleat located a little way aft of it. A bow line has to go forwards. To ensure the lead is correct, always go to the furthest side of the cleat from the boat to keep it open and don't pull it too tight.

4 Tying off To make off a line to a cleat, take a turn around the base ('0'), followed by two crossing turns around each horn ('88'), then a second turn around the base ('0') to leave an '0880' shape. This grips the cleat well and allows an easily controlled release. It also leaves the tail pointing in the right direction to become a spring line.

5 Spring lines Once the bow and stern lines are secure, they can now be returned up to the mid cleat to become stern and bow springs. As many boats only have a single centre cleat, you may have to use a simpler '080' in order to leave enough space for the second spring to be made off here too.

6 Sweating in The spring lines should be nice and taut, so sweat them in by leaning on the standing part and taking up the slack. The second spring should have the full '0880' to keep it secure. Locking turns aren't needed if done correctly.

how to
USE A LIFEJACKET PROPERLY

Wearing a lifejacket is one of the most important things you can do to increase safety afloat but unless you wear and maintain it correctly, it won't work as well as it's meant to if and when you fall into the water. Any personal flotation device (PFD) provides buoyancy that helps keep you afloat. This is measured in Newtons and for most PFDs starts at 50N. However, from 150N upwards, it should be buoyant enough to turn you face up even when unconscious, greatly improving your chances of survival.

Here are three things you can do to improve the chances of your lifejacket functioning as it's meant to when you need it most.

1 CHOOSE A PFD THAT IS SUITABLE FOR YOUR BOATING NEEDS
Buoyancy aids are not the same as lifejackets as they only provide 50N of lift. However, they are great for any form of watersports where there is a good chance of falling in but still being able to swim, such as paddleboarding or kayaking.

Anything that involves you being more than an easy swim from shore needs a proper lifejacket with at least 150N of uplift, and in my view it really should have automatic inflation – the last thing you want to be worrying about is finding the inflation toggle. If you are of a larger build or likely to be wearing thick clothing then 150N might not be enough so consider a lifejacket offering a higher level of buoyancy – full offshore ones go up to 275N. Also think about the features you might need, such as a strong clip-on point, crutch straps, a water-activated light if you ever go boating at night, a sprayhood if you risk being caught out in bad weather or a holder for a personal locator beacon if you're venturing offshore. All are available if your budget allows.

2 WEAR IT CORRECTLY
The most important thing is that you wear it in the first place, so be sure to find one that's easy to put on, quick to adjust and comfortable to wear for long periods of time. While this sounds simple, some always seem to end up in a tangled mess, while others push your head forwards and cause neck pain, so I strongly recommend going to a well-stocked chandler and trying on the various shapes and sizes until you find the perfect fit.

For it to support you properly in the water, it needs to be adjusted to fit your build and the amount of clothing you are wearing – you can't just adjust it once and forget about it – so make sure it's easy to adjust. The main strap needs to be tight enough for you to just be able to fit a clenched fist inside, while the crutch strap (an essential extra in my view) must not allow the jacket to ride up over your head.

3 CHECK AND SERVICE IT
So many people just buy a lifejacket, wear it occasionally and chuck it in a locker without bothering to look after it. A few simple steps can greatly increase a jacket's lifespan and its ability to function correctly when you need it. If it gets damp, sponge off any salt with fresh water, hang it up and only stow it away when it's properly dry.

Take the time to read the instructions, open it up, discover what's inside and how it's activated, check the gas bottle is tightly screwed in place and the service dates have not expired. For leisure boating, it will normally require servicing every two years, but in the intervening years, I'd recommend opening it, inflating it manually (preferably with a pump to avoid moisture from your breath) and check that it stays inflated for 24 hours before repacking it. I spend a lot of time afloat so I unpack mine and check it all through at six-monthly intervals.

Do these three simple things and your lifejacket will give you years of reliable service and will be there to save you when you need it most.

1 Buoyancy aids vs lifejacket A
standard 50N buoyancy aid such as this one is great for close-to-shore watersports where there's a good chance of getting wet. They are easy to swim in and they don't need re-arming after use. However, they are not the same as a lifejacket as they won't keep you face up when unconscious.

2 Choosing a lifejacket When
buying a lifejacket, make sure it's easy to put on, comfortable to wear for long periods of time and that the buckle is simple for you to open and close as well as quick to adjust. Also check that the manual activation toggle is easy to find if the automatic trigger should fail.

3 Adjust to fit
If the jacket is too loose it won't support you and may slip off. You should just be able to get a clenched fist inside the main strap. It will need to be readjusted to fit if you add or remove a layer of clothing.

4 Use the crutch straps

In my view, crutch straps are essential. They need to be pulled reasonably tight so that the jacket doesn't ride up when you are in the water. In the worst case scenario, the inflated bladder can even push your head under the water if it's in the wrong position.

5 Without crutch straps

If you don't use crutch straps then the jacket rides up and your body hangs below. If the main strap is also loose then the jacket can end up above your head and your airway becomes compromised.

6 Yearly checks

Ensure you check the date on the auto-inflation mechanism and that the bottle is tight in the holder, then inflate the jacket with a pump and repack it, making sure the manual inflation toggle is available.

how to
LICENSE AND USE A VHF RADIO

When you are new to boating or the boat is new to you, one of the first things you need to do is license the VHF radio to you, the owner. VHF licences are free – you just need to go to www.ofcom.org.uk and search 'ship radio'. You will also need an operator's licence for at least one person aboard, usually the skipper. This is administered by the RYA (www.rya.org.uk), who can advise you where to take the relevant course and exam. Licences for both vessel and operator are about the only part of UK boating that is compulsory.

Your radio licence will have two pieces of vital information – your Maritime Mobile Service Identity (MMSI) and Call Sign. The MMSI is a nine-digit number that identifies your radio and means that if you send a digital message the recipient can identify who it's from. The Call Sign is the second method of identifying your vessel. Displaying both of these prominently on your boat near the radio set is a sensible idea in case any of your crew needs to use it. A printed-out procedure card with that and all the information needed to send a full Mayday message is even better.

Digital selective calling (DSC) needs you to enter the MMSI (just once, and it can't be changed) into your VHF for it to work correctly. Check that your VHF set is linked to a GPS source such as a chartplotter (some modern sets have their own GPS receiver built in) so that it can transmit your exact position too. If working correctly, your lat and long is usually displayed on the VHF screen or with a symbol. If your VHF set lacks a DSC function then it's good practice, to have your lat and long viewable on a plotter screen or a GPS unit at all times so anybody aboard can call it out.

How to use a VHF radio correctly is an essential boating skill; you don't want to be fumbling about trying to remember the training when you really need it. You, as skipper, should have a good understanding of how it works, how to adjust it and how to send an emergency message. Ideally, at least one other person aboard should also have a working knowledge of the basics. For local boating (and as a back-up), a handheld radio might be enough, however a fixed set has more power and better features, and when combined with a taller aerial, will allow you to receive and transmit over a significantly longer distance.

The first thing you need to know is how to turn it on – many newer sets are not as intuitive as you might think. Once on, turn it up to half volume so there is something to listen to, then adjust the squelch. Turning the squelch up reduces unwanted background noise but also reduces its sensitivity, so aim to set the squelch as low as possible to maximise its reception. Be sure you do this every time you venture out.

Speaking into a VHF also requires practice; try to speak louder, slower and enunciate your words so that everything you say is as clear and precise as possible. The DSC function is similar to sending a text message except that the text is already composed, you just choose who to send it to. The red distress button on the face plate of most modern radios simply requires pressing for five seconds for it to send a Mayday message to All Stations, including the coastguard. The message contains your MMSI, GPS position and time; using the menu function, you can also add a reason for the distress, such as fire, sinking etc. This

Mayday DSC transmission must now be followed up with a spoken Mayday message, hence the reason for having a prepared card to make this easier. The DSC menu also allows you to carry out a radio check with a simple button push instead of having to trouble another vessel or coastguard stations. An almanac will have all the local channels for marinas, ports and other facilities. Get to know your set and your area so that you become comfortable using it. It's a really helpful tool as well as a vital piece of safety equipment.

1 **Licensing** These two licences make it legal for you to have and use a VHF on your boat. The Ofcom licence is for the boat, the other is an operator's licence.

2 **Handheld or fixed** A handheld radio may be all that's required for local boating or as a back-up to a fixed set. This one has a built-in GPS receiver and a DSC function. However, a fixed set will have a better range.

3 **GPS link** Check to see if your VHF is connected to your plotter or another GPS source so that the emergency DSC function will be able to transmit your position. If linked, the screen should display your lat and long.

4 Position display If your set doesn't have DSC or hasn't been linked to a GPS, always have your position information on display somewhere else near to the VHF, such as in the corner of your chartplotter, so it is always to hand.

5 DSC Emergency button To activate the red DSC Mayday button, lift the cover, press and hold for five seconds. This will send a digital message to all stations, containing your position, time and MMSI details.

6 Loud and clear When using the VHF microphone, you need to speak slightly louder, slower and more clearly than normal so people can hear what you are saying, especially when it's windy on board.

how to
SET YOUR ANCHOR

An anchor isn't just a handy tool, it's also a vital piece of safety equipment. If used correctly, it can often remedy a tricky situation or at least prevent it from getting worse. So, knowing how to use it, where the electrical breakers are and how to deploy it manually if needed is vital to good seamanship.

The first thing you need to know is how deep the water is and what type of seabed lies under the boat. Sand,

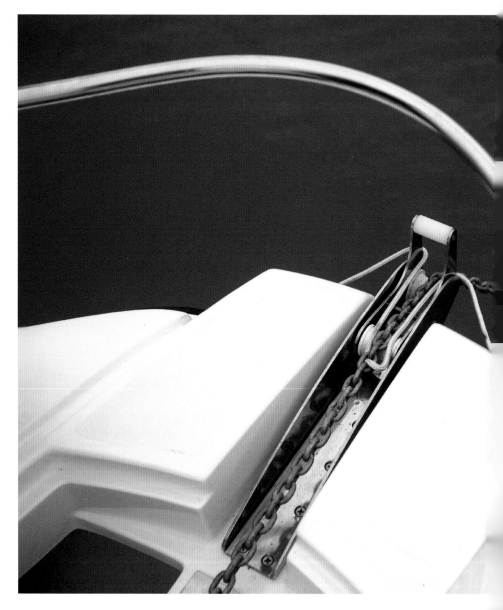

mud or shingle all give good holding, while weedy bottoms often prevent the anchor from digging, so if visibility allows, look for a sandy patch. Rocky seabeds can have fantastic holding but often make it extremely difficult to get the anchor out again.

How much rode (anchor line or chain) you put out depends on whether it's all chain or a mix of rope and chain. If it's all chain, four times the depth should be sufficient, if it's rope and chain then six times the depth is the norm. However, in windy weather or strong tides you will need to increase this.

If you're staying a while, you will also need to make allowance for the tide, so base your calculations on how much you will need at high water and make sure there will still be enough depth to stay afloat at low water. Marking your chain with different-coloured cable ties at set intervals will make it much easier to see how much rode you have put out.

To set the anchor, balance the boat against the wind and tide at your chosen dropping point, then gradually let out the chain while allowing the boat to drop back with the elements. I find that doing this in two stages helps to set it. Let out half the chain while the boat drifts back and wait for the bow to get pulled round, indicating it has set. Once it's holding, gradually let out the second half, giving it time to stretch out along the seabed rather than dumping it in a pile, then engage astern gently to make sure it has set. The chain should go taut and feel firm to the touch rather than vibrating, which indicates it's dragging. When you go back into neutral, the boat should move forwards as it takes up its place. The final step is to take transits to gauge if you're dragging, then use the chain lock or set up a bridal to take the weight off the windlass.

To retrieve the anchor, move the boat towards the anchor's resting place using the engines rather than the winch to avoid putting strain on the windlass. Lastly, when you get the chance, wash the anchor, winch and rode with fresh water to prevent corrosion.

1 Balancing the boat against the elements

Once you've selected your spot, face the boat into the elements and calculate the total length of rode you need to let out (four times the depth for an all-chain rode, six times for chain and rope). Now let out half the total rode while letting the boat drop back.

2 Lowering the chain

Pause after you've let out the first half of the rode and wait for the anchor to set, indicated by the bow of the boat being pulled around to face where it was dropped. Once this has happened, gradually lay out the second half of your calculated rode length to prevent it piling up in a heap.

3 Checking the anchor has set

Once the full length of your calculated rode has been let out, allow the elements to move you astern and then engage astern briefly to pull the rode taut and make sure it's not dragging. If you suspect it's dragging, place your hand on the rode to feel if it's vibrating.

4 Setting up a bridal

Once the anchor has set, use the chain stopper or improvise a rope bridal by threading a rope through the chain as indicated and attaching both ends to the two bow cleats. The idea is to take the weight off the windlass and prevent damage to the clutch and fittings.

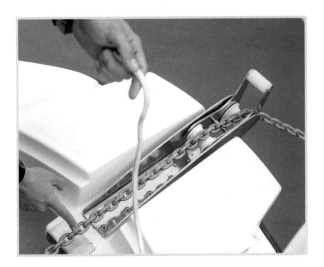

5 Taking the weight off the windlass

Once the bridal is set or the chain stopper is secured, let out enough extra rode to ensure the weight comes off the windlass and on to the bridal. If you anchor regularly, make up a bridal with a hook you can latch on to the chain rather than threading it through.

6 Retrieving your anchor

At retrieval time, the crew should give directions to the helm to enable them to move the boat towards the anchor under its own steam. This will ensure the anchor winch is only lifting the weight of the anchor and chain, not pulling the whole boat towards it.

how to
ANCHOR SAFELY

The anchor fitted to your boat isn't just a useful tool for enjoying a stopover in a pretty bay, it's also a vital piece of safety equipment that can prevent your boat drifting on to the shore in the event of engine failure. Even if the water is too deep for the anchor to reach the seabed, it will at least slow the rate of your drift.

In the case of a voluntary stopover, your first job is to choose a suitable spot to anchor. This can be from local knowledge, a pilot book, charts or even a digital plotter. Make sure there are no local anchoring restrictions or cables it could snag on, then check the charts to see what the seabed is made of. Sand, mud or a combination of both with shingle can all give good holding. Weed can make it tricky for the anchor to set and hold fast, while rock can give a fantastic hold if you catch it right but may also mean that it proves difficult to recover the anchor.

Next, determine how deep the water is. I suggest allowing four times the depth for chain and six times for a mix of rope and chain mix, more if staying overnight or it's windy. It's a good idea to mark the rode at 5m or 10m (16.4ft or 32.8ft) intervals with different-coloured cable ties so you know how much you are putting out.

In tidal areas, you also need to allow for any rise or fall during your stay. Make sure the spot you choose is not too close to other boats and if staying for a while you won't swing into danger due to a change in the wind or tide. When you've chosen your spot, release the anchor-securing mechanism – don't rely on the winch alone to keep it secure – then lower the anchor while the boat is facing into the elements. As the anchor drops to the seabed, keep the boat relatively still, then from the moment enough rode has been let out for it to touch the seabed, allow the boat to drop back naturally with the wind and tide while gradually letting out more rode. If the conditions are very light you may need to go gently astern to lay the rode on to the seabed.

The next step is to make sure the anchor has dug in, so either make it fast on a cleat, or lock the winch, and reverse at tickover so that the rode goes tight. A couple of seconds' pull is enough – then watch or feel the rode to check you have no juddering or vibration. If it is vibrating, the anchor is dragging, so either let out more rode and try again, or up anchor and start again. If there's no juddering, release the power, let the rode relax and the boat will end up in a settled position.

Now you need to check your exact position so you can spot if you are dragging, so look around and take some transits; one to the side and one fore and aft are ideal but your proximity to surrounding objects and an anchor alarm on the plotter can also help. Now let

everybody else know you are anchored by raising a black anchor ball.

Leaving is the reverse of the same process but remember that the windlass is designed to lift the anchor, not drag the boat towards it, so a nudge ahead to take the weight off the winch motor will help with retrieval. Make sure the anchor is stowed correctly.

Sometimes you need to control your boat's swing by using two anchors, either set in a V formation off the bow or one fore and one aft. This second 'kedge' anchor is often smaller, with a short amount of chain and a lot of rope to make it easier to handle. The technique is usually to make sure the main anchor is set properly, then let out a lot of rode to allow you to drop back before dropping the kedge astern then shortening up the main anchor rode as you let out the kedge rode, so you end up in the middle. For a V drop, often used for a long stay in variable weather, you again let the main anchor out with lots of rode and then motor forwards at a 60-degree angle to drop the kedge in line with but away from the main anchor before dropping back and tensioning them both so that you are held in a V shape.

Lastly, if you are anchoring somewhere crowded or are concerned about getting the anchor stuck, then having a tripping line attached to the 'wrong' end of the shank that is either brought back on board or tied to a float above the anchor is a good idea. When pulled from above, this tripping line helps dislodge the flukes, improving your chances of safely retrieving the anchor.

1 Anchor retainer

It's always advisable to have a method of keeping the anchor attached to the boat other than just the winch clutch. Here, we are using a clip on a short chain bolted to the deck.

2 Rode markers

Marking the chain with cable ties allows you to judge how much rode you have let out. I like to allow the anchor to touch the water and then mark the chain at every 5m (16.4ft) from that point on.

3 Setting a single anchor

Having dropped the anchor, use reverse to dig it in and check the holding. You should be able to see the chain tighten up and the bow dip as the anchor bites.

4 Twin bow anchors

To set two anchors in a V shape off the bow, set the main anchor, motor forwards at a 60-degree angle, then lower the kedge in line with the first, before dropping back to dig them both in.

5 Fore and aft anchors

To use two anchors set fore and aft, set the main anchor, then let out double the normal rode, drop the kedge anchor then pull in half the main rode so you end up lying between the two.

6 Using a tripping line

Adding a tripping line to the crown end of the anchor will help you to retrieve it. Add a small float to the tripping line to show others where your anchor's position is and avoid snagging it.

how to
RETRIEVE A MAN OVERBOARD

Someone falling overboard is a very worrying situation. There are so many factors that affect how serious it could get: water temperature, sea conditions, location, age, fitness, clothing, whether they are wearing a lifejacket. By far the best solution is to try to prevent anyone falling overboard by briefing crew on simple things such as holding on, wearing appropriate footwear, not leaving the cockpit underway and wearing a lifejacket. All of this helps but sadly man overboard (MOB) does still happen.

So, what should your priorities be if and when it does? How do you position the boat to get back to them, and if you are boating as a couple, how do you get your partner safely back aboard? I can't stress enough how strongly I advocate practising this eventuality, otherwise you won't know how to cope when it happens.

Your first action should be to slow the boat down, not in a mad slam-the-throttle-shut way, but with a swift reduction of speed. Now locate the MOB; they should be behind you and adjacent to your wake. Once you spot them, keep a close eye on them at all times – if you're alone in anything more than flat seas you can lose sight of them remarkably quickly. Your wake acts as a beacon, so make the best use of it while it lasts. Needless to say, if you can't spot them almost immediately, consider putting out a Mayday call or pressing the MOB button on your chartplotter and/or DSC-equipped VHF.

Assuming you can see them, turn the boat back towards them. You are going to use the wind to drift down towards the casualty, so turning upwind now (ie into the waves) will save time. Aim to stop at least 10m (32.8ft) upwind as a minimum, even more if it's windier. This will give you time to judge the boat's drift and grab a boat hook and line to assist with the recovery. The only reason I would ever consider starting closer than 10m (32.8ft) away would be if there were almost no wind or the casualty was face down.

Aim to keep the boat beam-on to the wind and waves, with the casualty level with the helm. You can use small clicks of ahead or astern to keep that position but be wary of using the engine when close alongside them. As you drift closer, try to judge their movement and yours so that the MOB ends up alongside at the lowest point on your craft, usually the stern quarter. I find a boat hook is the best thing to grab them with, then I like to pass

a line round them and tie it off so I can't lose them again. Now is the time to turn the engine off if there is any danger of it being knocked into gear.

Wet people are very heavy, so getting them out can be a challenge. If the casualty is able to assist, then deploying the bathing ladder or rigging a line from a cleat with a loop in it that acts as a step is your best bet. You could also use the hydraulic bathing platform if you have one or even get them to stand on the anti-cavitation plate of a large outboard motor while you raise it. If they can't help then you will have to drag them on to the platform. Keep your centre of gravity low as the last thing they need is for you to fall in too. If you can't get them out quickly, then that Mayday call will be essential.

1 Calmly reduce your speed

Slow the boat down, using your wake to help spot and locate the MOB. Then turn upwind to come back around towards and to windward of them.

2 Bring the boat to a standstill

Stop at least 10m (32.8ft) upwind of the casualty and roughly in line with the helm position. The boat should be parallel to the waves with the wind blowing across it. Here, I am indicating the MOB with the boat hook.

3 Let the boat drift towards

them Control the boat's drift so the MOB ends up alongside its lowest point. Crucially, the boat is sheltering the MOB from the wind and waves.

4 Grab the casualty

Once they are almost alongside, use a boat hook to grab the MOB. Note how I am keeping my centre of gravity low to ensure I don't fall in.

5 How not to do it!

My body position is too upright, which means the weight of a person pulling on the hook could drag me overboard. I should be crouching right down.

6 Connect them to the boat

Having pulled them close to the ladder, use a line to secure them to the boat before attempting to lift them out, just in case they fall back in.

how to

PICK UP A MOORING BUOY

On pages 100–101, we will learn how to hold our boat steady by balancing it against the wind and tide. A mooring buoy is the perfect place to practise this and prepare you for the next step of picking the buoy up.

First, look how surrounding craft are lying to buoys and approach from a similar angle. Bear in mind that all craft will sit at slightly different angles.

Hang back from the buoy by at least a boat length so you can establish your balance angle and work out how quickly your boat is responding to the elements. Once nicely balanced, you can begin your approach, keeping your speed low so your crew has time to pass clear instructions on the buoy's precise location. Successful mooring buoy work relies on good communication with your crew as the buoy is likely to disappear from the helmsman's view as you approach it.

You may be able to communicate verbally but I prefer to use hand signals as the person on the bow is usually facing away from you and their voice is easily lost in the wind.

Different buoys have different attachment means. Some have a pick-up loop you can grab with a hook and secure to a cleat. On larger motor boats, the bows are often too high off the water, so you may need to reverse up to it or use a lasso to drop around the buoy and lift it up to boat level.

Reversing up to the buoy also works well for buoys that just have an eye on the top to attach to, as the person on the bathing platform can more easily thread a line through it. For short stays in calm weather, you can simply rig a line from the stern but for longer stays you may need to rig a long line all the way from the bow to the bathing platform, taking care to ensure it runs outside all the rails. Balance the boat stern to the buoy, reverse slowly towards it, thread the line through the eye and walk it from the stern back to the bow, pulling on the line as you walk to rotate the boat so you end up secured bow-on. Careful use of the bow and stern thrusters can aid this process on a heavier boat.

1 Observe other boats

When selecting a mooring buoy, look how other craft are lying to the wind and tide, then aim to approach it from a similar angle. This should give you the best chance of balancing your boat against the elements for a slow, controlled approach.

2 Communicate clearly

As you get closer, the crew needs to give clear and concise instructions or hand signals on the direction and distance to the buoy. The last 3m (9.8ft) are crucial as the helm loses sight of the buoy beneath the bow and becomes totally reliant on the crew's instructions.

3 Hold steady

Once the pick-up buoy has been caught by the crew, the helm must keep the boat on station so no extra weight is placed on the line while the crew works to secure the line. Use a side transit to judge your position and a soft touch on the throttles.

4 Lasso the buoy

To lasso a buoy, make a large loop in the rope and throw your arms high and wide over it rather than aiming down at it. Allow time for the rope to sink around and under the buoy before attempting to lift it up. Again, the boat needs to remain stationary.

5 Reverse up to the buoy

Reversing up to the buoy is often easier for the helm because the view is better. It's also simpler for the crew because they are at the same height as the buoy. Be careful not to trail any lines that could get caught in the props.

6 Rig and secure a line

For relatively short stays, you can secure a line from a stern cleat but for longer ones, run a bow line outside the rails to the stern. Once you've threaded it through the buoy's eye, walk it forwards so the boat spins around and ends up secured by the bow.

how to
PICK UP A MOORING BUOY SOLO

Visitors' mooring buoys are likely to become a lot more prevalent in the years ahead due to concerns about possible anchor damage to sensitive eco-systems, so it's worth knowing how to pick one up even when cruising single-handed or with guests who aren't yet up to crewing duties.

First, you need to rig your boat for whichever end you wish to tie up by – a stern line is fine in sheltered waters for a short stop but in anything more than a light wind you will want to lie bow to the buoy. As the bow is much lighter than the stern and gets blown around more easily, it can be quite difficult to hold it still enough to get a line attached, even with crew to help.

Single-handed, it's harder still as by the time you have left the helm and made your way to the foredeck, the bow will have blown away. Additionally, the current trend for ever taller, more voluminous boats means it can be quite a stretch down to the buoy. As a result, and especially if single-handed, a stern-first approach works much better. The boat is more stable and tends to hold its position for longer.

To make that work, you first have to rig a line that is long enough to reach from the bow cleat to the stern cleat but not so long that it could get tangled in your props if you drop it. Make sure you pass it outside any rails, fittings and antennae before looping it around the stern cleat. I usually choose the side of the boat that gives me the quickest and easiest route from helm to stern cleat, unless it doesn't give me a clear view of the buoy as I approach it.

Having prepped the line, you now need to get your stern close enough to the buoy for you to thread it through. There are two approach techniques. The first is to position your boat downwind of the buoy with your chosen stern quarter cleat aiming at it, then use small nudges of astern to move towards the buoy, judging when to leave the helm with the throttle in neutral so that the boat's momentum carries you just close enough to reach the buoy. The alternative method is to approach bow-first but just before reaching it, turn and swing the boat around so the bow drops downwind and

the stern almost touches the buoy. Then, just before it passes it, a click of astern will stop the boat dead and allow you to walk aft.

Once you're at the stern, grab the buoy with a boat hook or by hand and thread the line through the top ring or pick-up warp. If it's windy, the weight of the boat will come on to the line quite quickly, so a good tip is to temporarily tie it to the stern cleat to take the load, wait a few moments for it all to calm down, then give a good pull to remove the weight and give you some slack. Now remove it from the stern cleat and walk forwards, pulling the line as you go so that the boat spins around and you end up with your bow to the buoy and wind.

Be prepared to take the weight of it as you make your way along the side deck, especially if it's windy, by keeping your centre of gravity low. Once at the bow, make sure you don't catch the line on the anchor, then tie it off either on the same cleat that you started from or the opposite one to create a bridal. When you're ready to leave, just untie the line and pull it through to release the buoy.

1 Approach the buoy First, rig a line from bow cleat to stern cleat outside all the railings, then reverse towards the buoy from down wind/tide. I made the initial approach bow-first then swung around and reversed the final metre.

2 Thread the line Grab the mooring buoy and pass the bow line through the top ring or mooring warp. I have laid the bow line down the starboard side of the boat so that it won't catch on anything when I take it back up to the bow of the boat.

3 Stern-to mooring If you're making only a short stop you can just rig a stern line directly through the mooring buoy's top ring and back on to the stern cleat.

4 Take the line forwards For longer stays, walk the line forwards, keeping your centre of gravity low and pulling gently on the line as you go to help the boat swing around.

5 Secure the bow line Once you are at the bow, you can either tie the line back on to the same cleat or take it around the anchor in order to create a bridal.

6 Sit back and relax Let the boat gently rotate so that it lies securely bow to the wind and buoy. Rigging a bridal allows the boat to sit directly in line with the buoy.

how to
USE A LOCK

Locks are used to move boats up or down to different water levels and due to swirling currents and winds, can prove tricky to negotiate, particularly for the less experienced boater.

Locks generally come in two varieties: those where you tie up to the lock wall and have to adjust your lines as your boat rises or falls, and those that have a floating pontoon inside that rises and falls with you.

Many locks are self-service, so consult the local guidebook for details of how they operate. On approach, be ready with

suitable lines and fenders – the latter may well need to go at gunwale height. If the lock is manual, you may need to come alongside the waiting pontoon and set the lock to allow your boat to enter.

Wind generally swirls around a lock entrance and if it's blowing across the entrance, you may well find the wind inside is actually blowing in the opposite direction. Be prepared for this as your nice blown-on berth can suddenly become a blown-off one.

The entrance can also be affected by swirling currents so whenever possible, let the water movement subside, then helm the boat positively into the lock. Always aim for the far end as this will keep the boat straight.

As soon as half the boat is inside the lock, knock the throttles back to neutral for a moment to ease your momentum and check the space you have chosen is still suitable before advising and instructing your crew accordingly.

Once alongside, either pick up the lock's lines or place your own around the nearest bollard or ring and bring them back on board. Take a single turn around your boat's cleat then hold the tail by hand so that the line can't get caught and jam. The idea is to gently adjust the lines as the boat rises or lowers. Going down in the lock is potentially more hazardous as any line made fast will quickly become load-bearing and impossible to release, so always carry a sharp knife just in case. Going up is simpler as you just keep bringing in the lines as the water rises. Only use one line per cleat and one line per task.

When it's time to leave, wait until all the water movement has subsided, then pull in your lines and gently ease away from the walls.

If you don't have a bow thruster, use a short stern spring to move the bow out before letting it slip, then move into the centre of the lock and focus on something ahead in the distance to keep the boat straight as you motor out between the lock gates.

1 Prep the boat
Position the fenders high up on the rubbing strake, ready for a lock with no pontoons. It's good practice to rig fenders on both sides, so you can choose where to berth if the lock is crowded or you get the manoeuvre wrong. Many locks have lines for you to pick up but keep your own lines close to hand just in case.

2 Entering the lock Drive positively through the entrance, keeping your eyes on the far end of the lock to help keep the boat straight. Be prepared for swirling winds or currents to push you off course; you may need to change plans and moor up on the opposite side to the one originally intended.

3 Securing the boat A single turn around the cleat with the crew keeping some tension on it is the best way to hold the boat on station – any more turns and the line can jam. Watch for anything getting snagged and carry a sharp knife just in case!

4 **Going up** This lock is being filled by the underwater sluices as well as a slight gap in the upstream doors. Keep the lines taut on board so you don't get slewed around. In this instance, we have used a stern line and a short breast line to hold the boat in place.

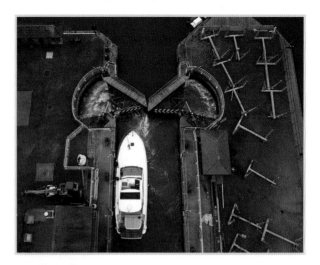

5 **Going down** Always make sure you have a person on each line, which is simply looped around the cleat with tension created by hand pressure only. As the boat drops, ease the line out, keeping just enough tension on it to hold the boat against the wall. This lock has ready-fitted long lines but take care when exiting not to leave them lying in the water, where they could be snagged by a boat's propellers.

6 **Ready to leave** Wait for the lock gates to open fully and the water movement to subside. When you're ready to leave, place the bow line back onshore, then pull gently on the stern line to move the bow away from the dock, then drop the line and move away.

boat maintenance

how to

ANTIFOUL A BOAT

Contrary to many boat owners, antifouling is one of my favourite off-season jobs. If done well, it will ensure you get a full season's boating with very little fouling and minimal loss of performance or fuel economy – even a small amount of fouling can increase fuel use by 20 per cent or more.

Most (but not all) antifoulings are toxic to certain forms of marine life but they can also be harmful to humans, so you will need personal protective equipment before starting. At a minimum, I'd suggest overalls, gloves, a face mask and a hat and goggles for working under the boat, but make sure you read the paint tin and hazard sheets for further guidance.

Most boatyards pressure-wash the bottom of the boat for you when they lift it. This will remove most of the growth from the hull, props and drives but make sure you wash off any barnacles or slime they may have missed, especially in awkward-to-reach areas, such as bow thruster tunnels and behind chines.

Our test boat came out reasonably clean and simply needed a good scrape with a sharp-edged scraper around the waterline to remove irregularities from the previous year's antifoul, followed by some 40-grade sandpaper to key the surface for the new paint. This is the moment when the mask and goggles are very important, due to the dust sanding produces. You need to be extra thorough around rough patches of old paint or areas that may have been missed, such as where the lift's slings or support chocks were. If the previous layer of antifouling has started to lift or flake off, you will need to scrape it right back to the gelcoat and key and prime it again. Lastly, rinse off any areas you have sanded and allow them to dry properly.

The next task is to mask off the waterline, so as to leave a nice clean edge, and around any metal outdrives or outboard mountings, taking care to leave a 2.5cm (1in) gap between the paint and the metal to prevent the copper compounds in the antifouling causing galvanic corrosion of the aluminium alloy.

Before applying the antifouling, I leave the pots upside down for 30 minutes so that all the heavier active ingredients aren't stuck at the bottom, then give it a really good stir for 5–10 minutes, making sure the stirrer reaches right to the bottom of the pot.

I also re-stir it each time I fill the paint tray. I find that a small paint roller with a high-density foam head is best for the main underwater sections as it gives me more control than a large roller but is still quicker, smoother and gives a more even thickness than a brush. However, I use a brush for greater accuracy along the waterline (working away from the edge of the tape), around the hull fittings and along the inside edge of the chines.

Unless the boat is huge, I go around the whole waterline first, working down to the first chine, then complete the hull underneath, by which time the paint around the waterline is dry enough for its second coat.

A good even coat that hasn't been rolled out too thinly is essential. The tin will say what the coverage should be so use it exactly as recommended – don't skimp. Most advise at least two coats (antifoulings are designed to wear away gradually over time to reveal fresh biocide beneath) but I often add an extra coat around the waterline and other areas of high wear. I like to lift the tape off after coat one to check that I have a good edge before applying more tape for coat two. This is also a good time to ask the boatyard to reposition the support chocks so you can fill in any areas that you couldn't get to during the first coat, although some boatyards prefer instead to touch these in when they lift the boat for re-launch.

Once complete, and having used up any paint left in the tray, I dispose of the brushes and roller heads safely, then go

about removing the waterline tape. My sneaky tip here is to pull the tape from the end you started taping with first so that all the overlaps are picked up and you end up with one long, continuous piece that you can roll into a ball, then tuck into the centre of your glove as you remove it, ready for convenient disposal.

1 **Masking up** Take your time and use good-quality tape – it sticks well and unlike cheap tape, it is easy to remove, leaving a clean line and no residue. Start from one end and overlap where needed. Don't forget to leave a gap between the antifoul and metal fittings, such as sterndrives and trim tabs.

2 **Preparation** Use a scraper around the waterline to remove any old lumpy paint – the tape is marking where the old paint finished. The best scraping technique is to apply gentle pressure on the head whilst drawing the scraper towards you. If you damage the tape, reapply before painting.

3 **Key the hull** Now go over the hull with coarse wet and dry paper to key the surface. Some yards only allow wetted paper, which reduces the dust but means you will need to wash off the residue before painting.

4 Start with the waterline Use a brush for the waterline and work away from the top edge. I also use a brush along the inside edge of the chines and around any hull fittings or engine mounts to avoid over-painting.

5 Roller the hull Using a small roller for the main hull allows better control and more even delivery than either a large roller or brush. Don't skimp on paint – follow the recommended coverage from the manufacturer.

6 Roll the tape up Once you've applied at least two generous coats, remove the tape in one go, pulling from the end you started at and rolling it into a ball as you go. When complete, tuck the ball into your glove, ready for disposal.

how to
POLISH A BOAT

Polishing a boat is an arm-aching but ultimately very satisfying task. What many people don't realise is that that polish isn't just an aesthetic nicety, it's also a vital extra layer of protection for the gelcoat that forms the outer skin of your boat's hull and superstructure.

A GRP surface, especially one that has been allowed to get dirty or chalky, looks like the surface of the moon when viewed under a microscope, with pitting, small craters and other surface irregularities that encourage further degradation. Some of this is inevitable as the gelcoat gradually fades and wears over time but you can help counter this by regular cleaning, polishing and, if needed, careful use of a cutting compound to remove the worst of those surface imperfections.

The polishing part is particularly important as it fills in any minor surface irregularities, preventing dirt, dust and other air or waterborne contaminants from settling in the microscopic dips.

A second coat of polish gives further protection and helps maintain the shine by encouraging water to run off. The amount of cutting back and polishing depends on how poor the existing surface is. A very chalky, dull finish would suggest that it hasn't been polished for a while. If left untreated, this can lead to longer-term damage that would require serious cutting back or even repainting. Areas with rust marks around stanchion bases or cleats and algae staining around

the waterline are best treated first with an oxalic acid cleaner, such as Y10 gel, that can be applied with a brush and left for 15 minutes before being hosed off.

For a routine polish, the normal process is to wash the boat with a mild detergent to remove surface contamination, grease and grime, then assess whether it needs cutting back with an aggressive cutting compound or whether a much milder all-in-one cutting/polishing product will suffice.

Our test boat, which has a partly blue hull that shows every mark, needed a moderate cut back all over with extra attention to the blue parts, followed by a milder cutting/polishing compound that would restore the shine and protect it. Coloured gelcoats, particularly dark blue or red ones, tend to show any chalkiness earlier than white ones, so you may need to polish these areas at least twice a year.

If polishing by hand, which I prefer for small areas, you'll just need one soft cloth to rub the polish in and another clean cloth to remove it. If using a mechanical polisher, then you'll need an applicator head and a separate polishing one. The most important rule of using a mechanical polisher is not to allow the surface to get too hot. Keep the speed of the head slow and use a water bottle or spray to dampen the surface as you move along. Follow this with two applications of a pure wax polish to leave a good shine and protect the cleaned surface underneath.

On this 9m (30ft) boat, the whole process took the best part of two short winter days, taking care to wear overalls, gloves and safety glasses when using the mechanical polisher.

Access to all parts of the boat was possible with a simple two-step ladder but larger craft may require longer ladders or even a platform to maintain a safe working height. Once the whole process is finished, it's good practice to rinse the boat off to remove any residue and leave it ready for launching.

1 Essential equipment You will need gloves, rust mark remover, deep cutting agent, combined cutting/polishing compound, two types of wax polish, water to keep the surface damp, tape to mark out the application area, rags and a mechanical polisher.

2 Washing down Wash the entire boat with a mild detergent, then treat any rust marks or algae stains such as these with an oxalic cleaner. Paint it on with a brush, leave for a few minutes to bleach out the stain then wash it off to remove any traces of the acid.

3 Cutting back Darker hulls show up chalkiness more than white ones. This one needs cutting back with a medium compound to remove the faded areas and take it back to the original gelcoat finish.

4 **Cutting and polishing** For small areas, apply the compound by hand on a cloth and rub it in with a circular motion, then polish it again with a clean, soft cloth. For larger areas, a mechanical polisher will make the job easier.

5 **Spot the difference** I masked off this section so you can see the effect of the cutting agent. This was done using the polisher on slow with light pressure and regular splashes of water to keep the surface damp.

6 **Polish and wax** This is the same area after applying a combined cutting/polishing agent, then two coats of polish. This should last the season on the white areas but will need repolishing after six months on the blue areas.

how to
CHANGE ANODES ON AN OUTDRIVE

For owners of outdrive boats, the annual lift-out is always greeted with some trepidation. Outdrives are complex pieces of machinery that offer boaters excellent performance and economy but which can be costly to repair as they get older.

The trick is to maintain them properly – don't skimp on servicing or anode changes or it could cost you a small fortune – and always take the opportunity to inspect and replace any items that show signs of wear whenever your boat has a lift-out. The bare minimum I would suggest doing every time your boat comes out of the water is as follows:

Anodes

Your boat has sacrificial anodes to limit the corrosion on submerged metal fittings. My boat has them on the outdrive, trim tabs and bow thruster. You can tell they are working as they will be pitted from corrosion. When 50 per cent worn, they should be replaced, especially if the boat is going to be afloat for longer than it has taken the first 50 per cent to disappear.

Some anodes come with pads that go between the anode and the surface of the trim tab to stop corrosion of the actual trim tab. Replace these as well. Whilst you're doing this, lower the trim tabs to their fullest extent so you can clean off any growth on the rams before trimming them all the way up again.

The outdrive anodes are a bit more involved. There is usually a bar anode set in front of the outdrive leg, which you can access by lifting the leg first. There is also a pair of small triangular anodes in the corners of the outdrive frame, two larger round ones on the cavitation plate, and a ring anode just forward of the propellers. To access this, you need to remove the propellers with a special spanner. While the props are off, it's good practice to inspect the sealing rings on the propeller shafts. If any fishing line gets caught here it can damage the seals and allow water into the gear oil.

Gear oil

To check the gear oil, trim the leg fully down, unscrew the dipstick on top of the leg and dip the oil. As well as checking the level, inspect the oil for signs of emulsification. Replace the dipstick's rubber sealing ring with a new one before retightening it.

Bellows

Using a flexible clip drive, undo the drive shaft bellows (the top one) at the leg end rather than the transom end. As you ease the bellows off at the base, check for water drips. Any rusty water in the bellows and the leg will need to be removed for further investigation. When done, replace the bellows, making sure it's properly on all the way round and the orientation of the clip is correct. Whilst out of the water, I'd also take the opportunity to polish the propellers and re-antifoul the outdrive leg using a special non-copper antifoul that doesn't corrode the metal.

1 Tool selection

Make sure you have the right tools, materials and replacement anodes to hand before your boat is lifted. Note the propeller spanner (top left) for removing the propellers and the special aerosol antifouling paint for the outdrive.

2 Trim tab anodes

These disc-shaped anodes sit on top of the trim tabs to protect the metal. Simply unbolt the old ones and bolt on the new. While you're there, lower the tabs to their full extent and clean the rams, then repaint the tabs with outdrive antifouling (see Step 6).

3 Outdrive anodes

There are multiple anodes on a sterndrive. These cavitation plate ones are the most obvious but you'll also need to replace the bar anode and the corner anodes located on the outdrive transom mount.

4 Ring anode

Don't forget to change the ring anodes, too. Remove the propellers with the wrench, taking care to lay out the washers in a line as they come off, then replace the ring anode and put them back in the same order.

5 Don't leave it too long

The pitting on the old anodes means that this was the right time to replace them. Any later and they could have corroded through, fallen off and left the outdrive unprotected.

6 Outdrive antifouling

Paint or respray the outdrive with antifouling that doesn't contain copper compounds. I tend to use International Trilux or Hempel Ecopower. Prep the surface by gently sanding the old paint first.

how to
CLEAN TEAK

Teak decks look lovely as well as being hardwearing, grippy and gentle underfoot. The one downside to real teak is keeping it clean. To maintain that just-fitted look takes a lot of work, ideally with a weekly hose-down or a bucket of sea water and a gentle wash and squeegee off. However, for most of us, that frequency just isn't possible so a deep clean at the beginning and end of each season becomes even more important.

There are two golden rules when it comes to cleaning teak: first, never use a pressure washer as the power will strip out any softer wood; second, never scrub along the direction of the grain or you will wear away the surface and leave the black caulking strips proud of the worn wood.

Traditionally, thick teak decks were cleaned with a flat stone and a bucket of sea water by scrubbing up and down. Nowadays, the teak tends to be a lot thinner and there are easier methods that rely on eco-friendly soap solutions or chemicals to loosen the dirt and restore the colour. The latter usually involves a two-step process with an acid solution to loosen the dirt and bleach the wood, followed by an alkaline one to stop the reaction and restore the colour.

Techniques and safety are key here. The chemicals are harsh on skin and the environment so you need to protect yourself with waterproof overalls and gloves. Whatever cleaning process you use, the first step is to wash off any loose dirt and grit, then use a squeegee to remove excess water to leave a wet but not flooded surface. If using the environmentally friendly approach, apply a copious amount of the detergent to an area about 1m square (10.7 square ft) and then work it into the surface with a circular motion (never with the grain), using a sponge to start with followed by a pan scourer and then, and only if needed, a brush with reasonably soft bristles.

You should see the dirt lifting off in the form of a grey/brown-coloured scum, depending on how dirty the teak is. Give this a good rinse off with the hose on a shower setting, then repeat the whole process until the soapy suds coming off are white with no discoloration. A final rinse and a good squeegee to remove any traces of detergent should complete the job but check by wiping a wet cloth along the direction of the grain to see if any bubbles form on the surface. If they do, you need to rinse and try again.

The chemical approach is far more dramatic but it's strong stuff and needs to be treated with caution. Carefully read the mixing strengths (ours was 5:1) – if you make it too strong it can damage the wood and make the black caulking strips go sticky. Follow the instructions on the bottle.

The first step invariably involves applying the acid solution first and working it into the wood using a sponge or soft-bristled brush in circular motions. It takes far less effort than a detergent and don't be alarmed if the wood goes dark brown. Leave it for about 10 minutes for the chemicals to do their bit before giving it a good rinse with water and a squeegee.

Next, apply the alkaline solution with a sponge, working it into the wood. You should immediately start to see a dramatic bleaching action, although you may need to go over it twice to make sure you have worked the solution into every corner.

When you rinse this off, a golden sheen will show through the wood and whilst it's wet you will be convinced that you have done a much better job than a more labour-intensive clean with soap suds. However, after 24 hours, when it's all completely dry again, the end result tends to be much the same. The chemical clean may be a touch lighter and requires less elbow grease, but given the environmental benefits of the eco-friendly approach, please try this first.

1 Before cleaning
At the end of the season, teak tends to look like this. The wood in this picture is in good enough condition but a previous sealant has worn away allowing the dirt to penetrate into the grain and leave it looking green and patchy in places.

2 Detergent vs chemicals
Products like this Ecover soap are far better for the environment and your hands but require much harder work than if you use harsher chemical cleaning agents. Regardless of which you use, you will need a bucket, sponge, squeegee, pan scourer and medium-bristled brush.

3 Using an eco-friendly detergent
Always work the soap into the wood using a circular motion. Start with a sponge, then progress to a scourer and, if needed, a scrubbing brush. Work on a small area at a time. You may need to repeat the process until the suds stay white.

4 Using a two-step chemical cleaner

Much like a detergent, the initial acid solution needs to be worked into the wood in a circular motion, using a sponge and then a brush to penetrate the grain, but it won't require as much physical effort and only needs to be done once.

5 Applying part two

After waiting ten minutes for the acid to work its magic, sponge on the second alkaline solution. This neutralises the acid and reveals the bleaching effect of the chemicals that restores the golden colour of the wood.

6 The results

After 24 hours, and once the teak has been allowed to dry properly, there is very little difference between the eco-friendly method (left) and the chemical clean (right). The eco-route takes more time and effort but the result can be just as good.

how to
REPLACE FUEL FILTERS

All diesel-engined boats have a set of fuel filters for each engine. They remove any contaminants from the fuel system and keep your engine running sweetly, but even one fill-up of poor fuel or a gradual accumulation of dirt and water over time is enough to clog up your filters. The good news is that it's relatively simple to change the filters and there's every chance you'll need to one day, possibly whilst at sea, so it's worth having a practice in less-challenging conditions first.

Most fuel systems have a coarse filter – to remove water and larger particles or dirt somewhere in the fuel line – followed by a fine filter, usually on the engine. Fuel problems often show up as surging, with engine revs rising and falling, or hesitancy when you apply more throttle. If you experience this, first check for any water in the coarse fuel filter. This is usually done by undoing a small tap or screw at the base of the filter and draining off whatever has settled there. If only a small amount of water and contaminant comes out and it doesn't solve the surging then a change of the filter element itself may be needed.

To change the filters, first locate the fuel cut-off and close it. You will need a filter wrench for canister-style filters or possibly spanners for other types, clean cloths, new filters, diesel-proof gloves, and a container for the old filter and excess diesel.

Depending on the type of filter, you will either have to change the whole cartridge or the element inside it. The latter requires you to remove the top, carefully pull out the element and replace it with a new one, along with the rubber seals, then reassemble it. Opening any filter introduces air into the system, which needs to be bled out before the engine will run again. To do this, you need to find the fuel pump and its primer. Follow the fuel lines and, usually where they join the engine, you will find the fuel pump and the primer. A primer is just a manual way to pump fuel. It can be a lever, a push button or even a wheeled knob that you unscrew and pull out like a mini bicycle pump.

Once you have located this, keep following the fuel line until you find a second filter. This is the fine filter and is usually a replaceable canister. On the top of the filter housing you will find a bleed point. This is likely to have been done many times before so will normally be the nut with the paint missing. Undo this about a quarter of a turn, then pump the primer until all the air has been expelled and clean fuel spurts out of the bleed screw. As soon as you get a steady stream of fuel, close it off. Cartridge-style filters are likely to need a lot more pumping than top-loading element ones, as the new cartridge will be completely empty of fuel.

That's the coarse filter changed and bled, so in theory the engine will now restart. However, if problems persist then you may need to change the fine filter. This is usually a replaceable canister-style filter just below the bleed point you found earlier. Some fine filters have a water-in-fuel sensor on the base that you'll need to unplug first. Now you can undo the cartridge using a filter wrench and screw in a new one. Don't forget to replace any sensors. Finally, bleed the air as before but pumping for longer in order to fill the new cartridge with fuel. You should carry spare fuel filters of both types on your boat.

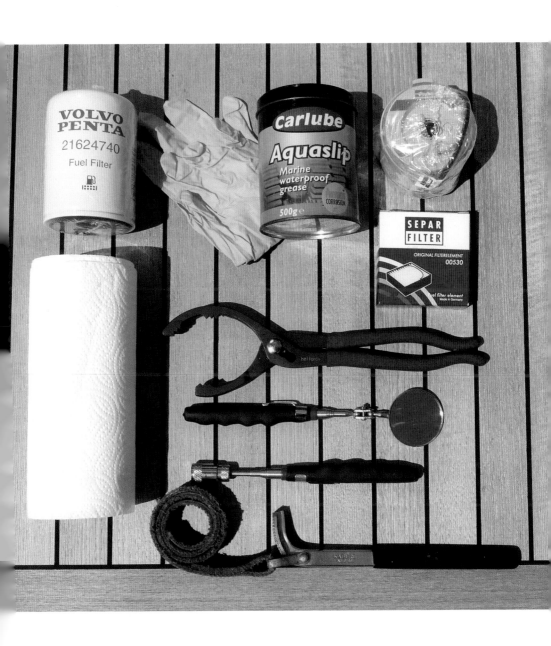

1 Shut off the fuel

With the engine stopped, pull the fuel cut-off lever and if possible check at the tank end that the valve is fully closed with the handle at 90 degrees to the fuel line (this one is open).

2 Carry the right tools

You will need a filter wrench, replacement filters, spanners, cloths, grease for the 'O' rings and a big enough container to catch the excess fuel and dirty filters.

3 Change the coarse filter

This is a typical coarse fuel filter with a replaceable element rather than an all-in-one cartridge. Open the top by unscrewing the T-handle or nuts (depending on the type), remove the element and seals, replace them with new ones, then reassemble.

4 Change the fine filter

These are usually mounted on the engine with a bleed screw or nut on the top and in this case a primer pump. Some also have a water-in-fuel detector on the base. Unplug any sensors, then unscrew the fuel canister for disposal and replace it with a new one.

5 Locate the primer pump

Primer pumps come in three main styles: levers that you wiggle up and down; buttons that you push in and out (as shown in this image); and plungers that work like a bike pump.

6 Bleed air from the system

Look for the nut with the paint missing, undo it a quarter turn, then pump the fuel primer to remove air and push clean fuel through the system until it flows out of the bleed screw.

navigation

how to

how to
SET UP YOUR CHARTPLOTTER

A plotter is often the first item people add to their new motor boat, sometimes at the expense of physical charts. Personally, I would not go to sea in an unfamiliar area without a printed chart. However, the reality is that many boat owners use some form of chartplotter as their primary form of navigation.

Used well, they are an excellent aid to navigation. However, coming straight from the manufacturer, they are just a means of establishing your boat's current position. How that is displayed and how you use that information is what keeps your boat safe.

So, for any boat I step on, I go through the following routine to ensure I understand what is being displayed and how it relates to me.

The first step is to establish the dates of any charts loaded on it. On start-up, most plotters display a warning, 'not to use this as your primary form of navigation', which most of us bypass or don't read in full. However, there is often a tab to 'read more' that should give the chart's date. This indicates how accurately you can rely on the information displayed. Next, I go to the set-up menu – some are easy to follow, others hide things in different layers and places so be prepared to explore. I then check the position shown to verify visually that I am where it shows me to be.

If I can find a signal strength indicator, I will check that too. You should be looking for a low HDOP of close to 1. This means that it's receiving a position and telling you accurately where you are.

Next up is system datum. Are the charts and plotter displaying position in the same format – usually WGS 84? I like the chart displayed in North Up, so the image looks the same as a printed chart, especially if I am somewhere unknown. Other people prefer a Head Up view, where the chart moves around with your direction of travel, much like most sat navs in cars. It's a personal preference.

Then I check the units being used and ensure it's in local time so that any tidal information is correct and not for another time zone. By the same token, if it's in an area with chart depths in metres, then I want the plotter to display the same. I use nautical miles and knots for distance and speed and if the plotter has a sonar, then metres for depth.

I like any bearings to be shown in True, again so they match the chart. Lastly, I look at the cartography – what is shown and how. Most units allow you to choose how much detail is available and give greater detail as you zoom in, unlike a physical chart, which only has what is printed on it. It's very easy to miss important information by being zoomed out too far.

On most plotters, you can also set the colours of different water depths. I like the chart to display deep areas in white, and shallow – usually below 5m – in blue.

If there is the option to show information alongside the chart itself I choose the following: position in latitude and longitude, course over the ground (COG), speed over the ground (SOG) and depth.

The crucial part is not to believe any of it without checking first. That means visual checks of your surroundings using the compass to see that the COG is roughly correct and the buoyage matches what the screen displays.

1 This is the set-up screen

of the plotter on our test boat – a Hybrid Touch version that pings up once you turn it on. Here, I have my finger on the settings button so I can check and adjust the key settings.

2 The settings

page allows you to configure units such as time, distance and speed to your own preferences. When the plotter is fresh out of the box, it normally comes programmed with land-based units, which will need to be adjusted to nautical ones.

3 Change the units

from miles into nautical miles and do the same for speed (knots) and depths (metres) so that they match your printed charts, taking particular care to use the same system datum (usually WGS 84).

4 Decide how much detail

you want. Some cartography displays have too much and look cluttered, while others adjust to how zoomed in you are. Choose with care what you leave out and check how zooming affects this.

5 North Up orientation is

the best for passage and route planning, however many skippers prefer to use Head Up when it comes to local pilotage as the chart view matches what you are seeing ahead of your boat.

6 Check how the bearing

and direction of the cursor are displayed on screen. Here, we can see that the cursor is on a bearing of 260T (True) and 2.14nm (nautical miles).

how to
CREATE A ROUTE ON A PLOTTER

On pages 79–81 we covered how to set up your plotter so that it shows the correct information in a format you are comfortable with when navigating. The next step is knowing how to enter a route and then use it to stay safe when underway.

If the area is unfamiliar, I always recommend using a physical chart first to plan where you want to go. It really helps to see your entire route in one go without having to scroll or zoom, and with practice you will learn to visualise in your head where things are in relation to one

another. This helps massively when you start to enter the route into the plotter, especially if you have a small screen and find yourself having to zoom in and out to see the detail for each potential waypoint.

In this example, I have planned a route around Poole harbour. It's not long or complicated and can be made entirely by eyeball with local knowledge but would be quite hard if you were cruising here for the first time.

The first step is to look at the chart, decide on the route, then using a pencil and ruler, mark the route from buoy to buoy or chosen position. Each change of course is called a waypoint and its position is marked on the chart using a cross with a square around it (the symbol for a waypoint).

Adding waypoints

Take a bearing of each leg using a Portland plotter, then measure the distance using a set of dividers. Write this information alongside each leg on the chart. You may prefer to write all the different legs down as a list for greater clarity, but I am happy with it just being on the chart.

The next step is to go to the boat's plotter and using the 'New Route' feature place the cursor at your planned starting position to create the first waypoint. Now move the cursor to the end of the first leg and press 'add waypoint'. Repeat this process for each leg of the route until the route is complete. Don't forget to save and name the route.

Before you run the route, it's a good idea to compare the route information on screen with what you have written on the chart. There will always be minor differences in bearing and distance as you are comparing pencil lines and analogue measurements with precise electronic ones and it assumes you have chosen exactly the same spot for each waypoint. However, any major differences should jump out, enabling you to correct them before setting off.

When you're ready to run the route, choose the route from the plotter's memory and make sure you are running it in the correct direction (most plotters give you the option of forwards or reverse). As you approach the first waypoint, select the route and press 'go'. Don't start the route too early or it will show the bearing of the first waypoint from where you currently are, which may not have clear water in front of you. Turn to pages 86–89 to see how it works.

1 Begin plotting

Draw the first leg on the printed chart using a 2b pencil (it should be easy to rub off afterwards) and mark the start and end with the waypoint symbol (a cross with a square around it).

2 Note the bearing

Rotate the plotter centre so the blue arrows align with chart North and read off the bearing of the first leg (here it is 296°T). Write this alongside the leg on your chart.

3 Note the distance

Use a set of dividers to measure the distance, then take it to the scale printed on the edge of the chart to see how far it is in nautical miles. Write this information on the chart too.

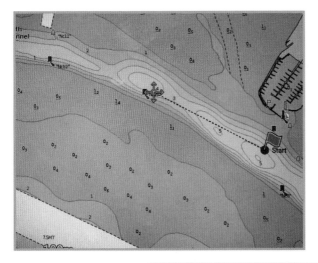

4 Transfer to the plotter

Now place your start point and each subsequent waypoint on the plotter by moving the cursor to the location and clicking on the spot. This is where referring to the printed chart really helps.

5 Route overview

This is what the completed route looks like on the plotter. The route direction can be seen from the arrows. We'll show you how to run the route on pages 86–89.

6 Compare both charts

It's now easy to compare the chart plotter's route list of distances and bearings with those you've marked on the chart. This allows you to check both sides match and the route is safe to use.

how to
FOLLOW A ROUTE ON YOUR PLOTTER

Having completed your plotter set-up (pages 78–81) and planned and entered your route (pages 82–85), now comes the part that all that preparation was for – actually running the route.

In theory, if the first two steps have been completed correctly, this should be a simple case of just following the pre-programmed information. However, as a navigation examiner of many years, I can honestly say I have seen many skippers struggle to interpret and check the information in front of them, even when they have actually planned it all correctly.

There are a number of things to be wary of but these are the ones that occur most often:

Waypoint arrival alarms – most systems allow you to adjust the range so that it activates at a sensible range of, say, 100m (328ft). If it's set too wide, ie 500m (1,640ft), it will say you are at the waypoint when in reality you still have quite a way to go. This can have serious implications, as it may not be safe to switch headings to the next waypoint until you are much closer to or even just past your chosen waypoint. Change heading too early and it may take you somewhere unsafe.

On a similar note, once the alarm has triggered, most systems switch to the next waypoint as soon as you press 'acknowledge'. If your waypoints are set close together, that might simply cause it to trigger again immediately for the second waypoint. So particularly in a congested area, like our planned route, it's important to have a tightly defined waypoint arrival alarm, and then make sure you are completely happy with your

location before changing heading. There is no problem with switching to the next waypoint early using waypoint advance if you are sure that you have completed all your checks.

Waypoint locations – a key factor when choosing your waypoint locations, and one to monitor closely, is where the next waypoint is in relation to the one you are about to arrive at. Will it involve a change of heading to port or starboard, by how much, and how far away is it? This is crucial as it allows you to be sure that the next waypoint bearing and distance given by the plotter actually matches what you are expecting. If well prepared,

you may already be able to spot your next waypoint, assuming you have used a physical object, such as a buoy, that is within visible range. I find that either using the ship's compass or a hand-bearing compass to sight along to the next bearing is a simple and reliable way to spot the next waypoint well in advance of the one I am currently heading to.

Some find using the plotter in Head Up mode makes this easier, but I personally prefer North Up as having planned the route on a chart I still have the correlation to hand and find it easier to spot errors. The distance part is used to allow you to judge how long the next leg will take, most plotters show this information as Bearing To Waypoint (BTW), Distance To Waypoint (DTW) and Time To Go to waypoint (TTG).

Tide and wind – lastly, when you plot a simple route with charts or enter it directly into the plotter you are making no allowance for any tidal movement of the water itself or any wind pushing you off your intended track. On short legs this is perfectly safe as long as you stick to your intended ground track. On longer legs you will need to closely monitor your progress and watch the course over the ground (COG) on the screen; if this is close to the bearing to waypoint (BTW) then you are heading in the right direction.

1 **Waypoint arrival** In this case it's easy to make a visual check of where we are as there are physical marks (port and starboard cans) on either side of the boat but it's important to check that the plotter and the chart match.

2 **The next waypoint** Here, I am using the ship's compass like a hand-bearing compass, sighting along it with my hand to where the next waypoint should be. This allows me to confirm where my next heading is before I make the turn.

3 **Keep a lookout** Not only do you have to follow your navigation correctly, but you also need to keep a good look out and give way when appropriate. It's easy to overlook what's going on around you.

4 Don't jump the gun
This is a classic case of the waypoint arrival alarm being over enthusiastic; it has jumped ahead to the next waypoint and is telling me to cut the corner when I still have some distance to go.

5 On your marks
It's crucial to make sure you have located the correct mark; here, we have a major channel mark (red can) and a smaller channel mark (red post). We want the smaller one for our turn to port.

6 On course?
I have switched to Head Up mode and can see that my Course Over Ground (COG) and Bearing To Waypoint (BTW) are reading between 112° and 114°. That means we are heading in the right direction.

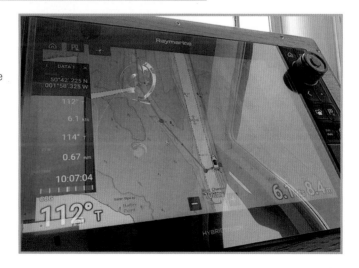

how to
USE PILOTAGE

Some people consider pilotage a dying art. Ashore, you can simply pop your destination into your car's satnav and off you go without a clue as to how it's getting you there. So long as you arrive at the correct door, it's fine.

The latest generation of chartplotters are heading that way too. However, there are two key differences that mean I can't see it happening too quickly: there are no roads to follow; and you're either afloat or aground, possibly on rocks. So, for me pilotage – the process of using land or sea marks to navigate your way into a port or harbour – is still an essential skill to have, with a long future ahead of it. The chartplotter is a wonderful aid in getting all that correct but the pre-planning is still essential.

Any pilotage exercise comes at the end of a passage, once you have arrived at your chosen waypoint (be it a navigation mark, headland or other identifiable feature) and you switch from passage-making mode to a more localised pilotage exercise. Then, your chosen route will use significant features, either natural or man-made, to guide you in.

I like to start with a chart and plot my intended route with waypoints. Then I draw the outline plan on a piece of paper. This allows me to visualise the essential points of the plan in my head in easy-to-follow steps. There is no right or wrong way of doing this, just the style of plan that works best for you. This could be a hand-drawn picture, a list of steps or simply a written plan. The crucial thing is that it must be clear and easy to refer to. I also like to add the light characteristics of any navigation marks I have chosen so the plan can be used at dusk or night-time as well. Do double check in the almanac and pilotage books carefully as some harbours have differing approach routes in the dark due to some marks not being lit.

Next, enter your plan into the chartplotter as well. This will allow you to reference what you are seeing through the windscreen with your handwritten plan and the chartplotter before deciding whether it's safe to proceed. I find that a hand-bearing compass is an essential bit of kit, not only for identifying the marks you are searching for by looking along the correct bearing, but also for identifying the next one before you get to the turning point, so the pilotage becomes a smooth exercise of precision. This also allows you to stop at any point on the route to identify your next mark before leaving the safety of the one you have already identified correctly.

Even the MCA have got in on the act and now have a mantra that is driven into every new cadet and captain. They call it APEM – Appraise, Plan, Execute, Monitor – plus they also like to talk about 'berth to berth' planning. Personally, I still like: Pilotage to leave, Passage in the middle and Pilotage to arrive, which seems more apt on smaller boats, where the passage can be influenced by so many different factors.

1 **Mark up the chart** Using a printed chart of the area, add your intended waypoints in pencil with the correct bearings between them. This forms the basis for your simplified pilotage plan containing the key information you need to keep you on track.

2 **Draw up the pilotage plan** I like to hand draw my pilotage plan. This allows me to simplify the chart so that it contains only the key information I need (bearings, nav marks, lights, depth contours etc) and how I am going to use them to keep me on my intended track into the port.

3 **Enter waypoints in a plotter** You can now follow the waypoints on the plotter while using your hand-drawn pilotage chart to cross reference. Relying solely on the plotter means you might spot errors too late.

4 Take regular bearings

My favourite item afloat is a hand-bearing compass. Use this to check that the nav mark you are looking at is on the correct bearing and to help you find the next mark before you need it.

5 Use navigation aids

Sectored lights are useful aids at night in a pilotage situation. If it's red then you are too far to port, if it's white you are on the right heading and if it's green you are too far to starboard.

6 Mark up light characteristics

It's good practice to add the light characteristics of navigation marks to your plan, even if you intend to arrive in daylight. That way, if you get delayed for any reason then you will have all the info to hand.

how to
SET UP A RADAR

Mention radar and most people think fog. Technically, fog starts at visibility of less than 1,000m (3,280ft) and significantly changes your responsibilities under the collision regulations, the most pertinent being that we all move from being either a stand-on or give-way vessel to ALL being give-way vessels.

Setting up your radar correctly is crucial to its performance and is best done in clear weather with visible targets so you can see the changes to the picture as you adjust the settings. It's important to do this before you encounter any fog otherwise how will you know it's working correctly? Settings are adjusted either with individual buttons or soft keys. The major variables are range, brightness, gain, tuning and sea and rain clutter.

The first one to adjust is range as it needs to be set relative to your location. In a harbour, half a mile is usually about right. Next up is gain, which adjusts the sensitivity a bit like squelch on a VHF; too much and the picture becomes a mass of targets, too little and things disappear. Tuning is next, and you are looking for a crisp image of a nice hard target.

Now try all that again at a different range; older sets often need adjustment with every range change. More modern sets usually have an auto-tune function but it's still worth seeing if this gives a better or worse picture than yours.

The final adjustment is for sea and rain clutter; sea clutter adjusts the return from waves – too little and small objects like navigation buoys can be lost in the mess of reflected waves close to the boat, too much and everything disappears – it's a delicate balance. Rain clutter adjusts how rain affects the picture, so heavy rain often appears as cotton wool-type blobs on the screen, so adjustment allows you to get some clarity through the rain.

Most leisure boat owners prefer to keep the radar screen in Head Up mode as all targets appear relative to the boat's heading. Personally, I find North Up easier for pilotage into harbours, especially unfamiliar ones, as the land will appear pretty much as it does on a chart. Be careful though – changes in tide height can make the land appear oddly shaped.

Help with judging how dangerous targets are to you and the potential risk of a collision is available via the Electronic Bearing Line (EBL). This works just like a steady compass bearing: if you place the EBL on a target and the target tracks down the line towards you – you will hit it! You may also get a Variable Range Marker (VRM), which gives an accurate distance to the target rather than just using the range rings. Many sets also offer a choice of modes – harbour, coastal and offshore – which adjust the type of transmission. Radar sets traditionally show a relative motion picture – where your motion relative to other boats is shown, and some more expensive ones will also allow true motion.

1 Setting it up

Turn on the radar and set it to transmit – most have a warm-up period of between 15 seconds and a minute. When ready, adjust the screen brightness and choose a range that's suitable to the area you are in.

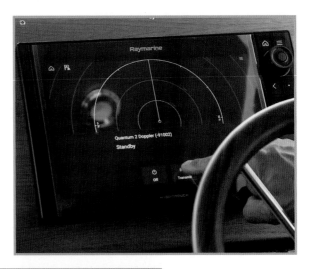

2 Adjusting the picture

This set has an auto-gain function, which actually works very well, but if you want to adjust it manually you can select 'adjust settings' from the menu and use the soft keys to tweak it.

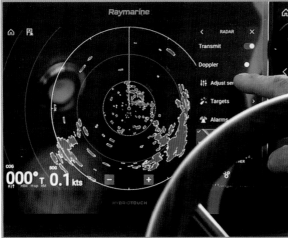

3 Too little gain

Dial down the gain too far and most targets vanish. The solution is to turn it up slowly until you get the right level of detail – most radars usually take a couple of sweeps to get it right.

4 **Too much gain** Dial the gain up too high and the screen becomes a mass of clutter and noise. Turn it down slowly, waiting for a couple of full sweeps between adjustments until the speckles have just disappeared.

5 **Collision avoidance** You can risk assess targets by clicking on them to set up an electronic bearing line (EBL). If the target consistently tracks down the line towards you, you will end up hitting it.

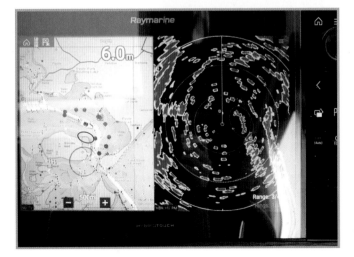

6 **North Up or Head Up?** The chart-plotter is showing North Up with Brownsea Island's harbour wall south of our boat. The radar is in Head Up mode and has the same contact to starboard – see the blue ovals on both screens.

boat handling

how to

how to
HOLD YOUR BOAT STEADY

Many people find skippering a motor cruiser challenging. The shallow hull form has limited grip on the water and combined with high windage, the boat can feel hard to control at low speed. This gets worse as the wind gets up and on good sailing days, many motor boats stay in the marina because their owners are too intimidated by the conditions.

All good boat handling comes from being able to balance the boat against the elements, ie what the wind is doing above the water and what the tide or stream is doing beneath it. Master this skill and you will be a calmer, safer boater

and buy yourself the time and space to plan any subsequent manoeuvre.

So what's the secret? Primarily, observation. The first step is learning how to spot what the wind and tide are up to, and then taking into account any local anomalies that might affect your boat. Wind information can come from

anything from patterns on the water to flags on neighbouring buildings or the top of yacht masts. Just remember that a yacht mast may be giving direction and strength 15m (50ft) up rather than the 0–4.5m (0–15ft) level that's affecting your boat. The wind also has a nasty habit of testing you with sudden gusts and changes of direction or by dying away when you're leaning on it. The chances of this happening also need to be taken into account.

Water movement is usually more constant and predictable, although you still need to look for any anomalies around obstructions that might redirect the speed or direction of flow. Having done your observations, you need to practise balancing the boat against these two elements. Even the best of us can only balance the boat with either the bow or stern pointing into the combined force of these elements. Many craft are more easily balanced stern to the elements, but most people find bow-on a better place to start as it's easier to spot what's going on and react accordingly.

The absolute key to judging what's going on is to use transits – that's two items that when lined up, are stationary in relation to each other. Any movement of these objects relative to each other means the boat is moving. You really need two transits, one off the bow if facing forwards (or the stern if facing aft) to judge which way you are moving laterally, and one abeam so that you can judge any movement fore and aft.

The boat is only truly stopped when both transits are static. The boat won't stay that way for long, so the next skill to practise is predicting which way it will be moved next by the elements, and being just ahead of that movement with your helm and engines to counteract it. Especially practise using the one abeam so that when you moor the boat, you can judge exactly when the boat has stopped completely.

1 **These pontoon posts** make a perfect transit, and the way they're positioned in the marina means they are ideal for an abcam transit to judge if the boat has stopped moving ahead or astern. At present, they're slightly 'open' or apart, and the gap between them should stay the same if the boat is stationary.

2 **The same two posts** are now perfectly in line and can be described as 'in transit'. It's now immediately obvious if the boat moves ahead or astern as both posts will once more become visible. With practice, you can anticipate this movement and use the gears to keep the boat still.

3 **Here, you can see the skipper's head** turned to watch the transit with his hands resting on the throttles in case he needs to give a nudge of ahead or astern to hold it there. You can still judge if you are stationary using the transit when it's slightly 'open' by having no movement of the posts relative to one another.

4 **Spot on for an abeam transit** You can see from the wash that the skipper has just used a short burst of starboard ahead to keep the boat in position 'on transit'. His next move should be a glance towards the bow to see that it hasn't been blown off course in the meantime.

5 **Now the boat is lined up** along the ahead transit using the starboard marker post and the breakwater. Again, you can see the skipper has just used port ahead to move the vessel on to the transit. He will then monitor this and the abeam transit to gauge what's needed next.

6 **Here we are stern to the elements** and the skipper is lining up the same two transits. Note that the vessel is sitting at a slightly different angle as the balance between wind and tide means that the vessel is less square on to the transit but easier to hold still using only small nudges of ahead and astern as required.

how to
TURN IN A TIGHT SPACE

Turning in a tight space is best broken down into a series of pre-planned steps. Even experienced skippers take a deep breath when presented with a very small space, especially if it's windy. So, it's best to practise when the conditions are not too challenging so that each step of the process becomes as smooth and controlled as possible.

First, as ever, carefully assess the turning area. Work out where the prevailing wind and tide are coming from and which way you are going to turn (it's always easier to turn towards those elements). Look for any craft that present an extra hazard by sticking out further than the rest and any empty spaces that might give you extra room. Remember the pivot points on your vessel – about a 1/3 from the bow in ahead and 1/3 from the stern in astern – because that means the remaining 2/3 of the boat will be prescribing a wider arc than you might imagine.

On approach, try to get your boat stationary and balanced against the elements (page 101). This will allow you to keep your speed as slow as possible. As you move into the area, keep monitoring the conditions as the wind will usually decrease when you pick up shelter from other craft, while any current will become slacker the closer you get to the shore. Allow for this with your approach angle and keep looking well ahead for any changes. Use clicks of ahead gear to keep your speed down.

When ready to turn, allow the boat to slow, then use full lock towards the up-element side of the area and engage ahead. Use the space ahead of you to full advantage – it's usually easier to see the bow than the stern – so go as close as you feel comfortable with. I find that using a couple of small clicks ahead is better than opting for one large one as it allows me to keep the speed slow.

Before the space in front of you gets too tight, go into neutral, reverse the wheel to full opposite lock and engage astern. Again, small clicks of astern are generally better than one larger one, allowing you to use all the space and keep the speed low. Be careful, though,

104

as this is the down-elements side of the area so you will be pushed this way quicker than the up-element side.

Before you run out of space, go back into neutral, reverse the wheel, engage ahead and drive out. If the boat has not completed the turn and there is not enough space to leave, repeat the last two steps until you have enough room to drive out, taking into account the stern's wider turning arc. As you leave, keep the boat angled slightly towards the elements so you don't get pushed into danger again.

1 **The approach**
Having worked out what the elements are doing (a gentle breeze on the starboard beam in this case), approach from a down-element position with your boat nicely balanced against the wind/tide and reasonably stationary at the start.

2 **The entry** As you enter, keep checking your balance angle (wheel slightly to starboard in this instance to counter the breeze) and use it to allow progress with a nice slow speed. Use small clicks of ahead and then neutral to keep the speed low. Keep slightly to the up-element side.

3 **Initiate the turn** When you're ready for the turn, use full helm (in this case to starboard) and engage ahead for a moment. Remember the stern will sweep a larger arc than the bow. Go into neutral as the gap closes.

4 Use the space
As this is the safer up-element side, use as much space as you can safely see. Then, whilst still in neutral, reverse the steering lock (in this case full to port) and engage slow astern to continue the turn.

5 Complete the turn
Use small clicks of astern and neutral rather than one larger one to go as far astern as you feel comfortable, then reverse the wheel (in this case full to starboard) and drive ahead to leave.

6 Stay up-element
Use ahead sparingly to exit back out into the main area. Stay towards the safer up-element side so that if any vessel appears you can slow or even stop without being blown into trouble.

how to
TURN A SINGLE-ENGINED BOAT IN A TIGHT SPACE

Executing a tight turn in a small space in a boat with a single engine is one of those challenges that makes even experienced skippers take a deep breath. However, with a bit of practice and by making full use of the available space while accounting for any wind or tide and keeping your speed as slow as possible, it soon becomes second nature.

When the opportunity presents itself to test your technique, choose an area roughly twice the length of your boat in which to practise – you can always try a smaller space once you've nailed it. Now identify what the wind and any tide or stream are doing, as these can have a big influence on the turning ability of your boat, especially if it has lots of windage and a planing hull (displacement craft tend to have deeper keels and larger rudders, giving them more grip on the water). You need to judge how much these factors will influence your boat in order to decide which is the safe side of the turning space. If you're still unsure of this, bring the boat to a halt before entering the confined area, using a transit to ensure that you have come to a complete stop, and see which way the elements push you – this then becomes the danger side.

Once you've determined this, your approach will always be easiest with your bow moving towards the safe side, so position your boat to enter the tight space with your bow pointing in that direction. This angle will change the further in you get as any stream and wind generally starts to weaken due to the shelter from other craft.

Next, choose your turning spot and, keeping the speed as slow as you can while still retaining full steering control, turn the wheel towards the safe side of the space while using a click of ahead

to push your bow up into that space. If you have judged it correctly the boat should now be almost stationary and facing into the elements. Next, by turning the wheel the other way and engaging astern, bring the boat back towards the danger side of the space with the elements.

When you have used as much space as you feel safe to, turn the wheel back the other way again and go ahead to push the bow back towards the safe side. If there's sufficient room you may be able to complete the turn. If not, repeat the manouevre until you can.

Having now practised judging which end is the safe side, the approach, the manoeuvre and becoming comfortable with when to swap helm direction and gear, choose progressively smaller spaces until you can cope with a space that is only slightly larger than the boat itself.

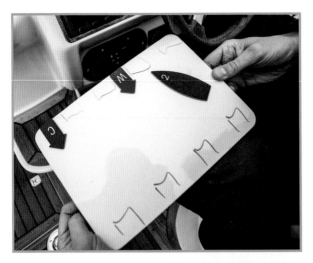

1 Work out the safe side Take stock of where the wind and current is pushing the boat. In this case, a reasonably strong current and a light wind make the top of the board the 'safe side'. Your approach into the space is a combination of angle versus speed.

2 Choose a start point This is the most crucial part of the whole manoeuvre; get the start point correct with the boat balanced and the bow facing into the safe side, and you stand the best chance of success.

3 Push the bow to the safe side Use gentle clicks of ahead to push the bow up towards the safe side of the space. Your ferry glide angle will become shallower the further in you go as the stream will reduce in strength.

4 Use all the space Keep the wheel pointing towards the top of that space (in this case to starboard) and move as far into it as you feel comfortable with, using the elements to slow you down and keep the boat balanced and almost stationary.

5 Move astern Turn the wheel the other way (to port in this instance) and use a click of astern to back away and give yourself room to complete the turn and exit safely. Don't be afraid to go astern further if you need more room to get the bow round.

6 Complete the turn Put the wheel hard over to starboard again and back into ahead to bring the bow round and allow a safe exit. Keep the bow on the safe side as you exit because the stream will become stronger as you leave the shelter of the moored boats.

how to
TURN A TWIN-ENGINED BOAT USING ONLY ONE ENGINE

There are two main reasons for buying a twin-engined boat: the first is redundancy (if one breaks, the second can get you home); the other is manoeuvrability (two engines give better control at low speed). That's all well and good until one engine does break down.

You may still be able to get home but berthing it has just got a whole lot trickier, so it pays to know how your boat handles on one engine.

As with any emergency tactic, it's best to have a go at this in advance, preferably on a calm day with plenty of space to play

in. The best way to do this is by learning how to turn your boat on one engine. If you can master this then you are half way to getting it into a berth.

Obviously, there are lots of single-engined boats that turn just fine with one engine, but it's mounted on the centre line with a single large rudder that steers equally well in both directions. Twin-engined boats have offset engines and two smaller rudders, so if one engine breaks it's always easier to turn in one direction rather than the other. If there is enough space to turn around using ahead only then

turn in the direction it wants to go, with the engine on the outside. That is also the case with steerable drives, such as twin outboards or sterndrives, even in restricted spaces. However, with a shaftdrive boat and only limited room to manoeuvre, it's easier if you steer the boat against the working engine. This is because there are three factors that affect the steering of a twin shaftdrive boat: prop offset (the further the propeller is from the centreline, the greater the steering effect), prop walk (the sideways travel all propellers produce, particularly in astern) and the rudders (these are more effective in ahead than astern due to increased water flow from the propeller thrust). Knowing these dynamics will help you use them to best effect.

If your port engine is dead, leaving just your starboard engine running, and you turn the boat to port (the way it wants to) you will have all three factors working for you – prop offset, prop walk and rudders. The moment you run out of space and go astern, they all start to work against you – the offset is on the wrong side, prop walk is pushing you the wrong way and the rudder is all but useless, so you'll end up back where you started.

The better option is to turn to starboard, against the working engine and use the rudder to overwhelm the other two. Going ahead, the offset is against you and so is the prop walk but you can overcome both of these with the help of extra revs to increase water flow over the rudders.

Once you have turned through the first 50 or 60 degrees, take the boat out of gear. Now there is no offset or prop walk to fight against but the flow of water over the rudders means the boat keeps turning. When you run out of room and engage astern, the prop offset and prop walk are now working for you. You don't even need to adjust the rudders as you won't be going astern quickly enough for them to have an impact. These two factors alone will drag the stern through the remainder of the turn, completing the 180-degree spin in a controlled manner. On pages 116–119 we'll cover how to get into a berth using only one engine.

1 Start the turn
With just the starboard engine working, position the boat well to port to give yourself maximum room to turn to starboard. Now increase the revs and use full starboard lock to initiate the turn and overwhelm the negative effect of the propeller offset and prop walk.

2 Engage neutral
Once you've completed around 50 degrees of turn, and with the wheel still hard over to starboard, bring the engine to neutral, killing the prop offset and prop walk but allowing the water flow over the rudders to keep the boat turning.

3 Use all the space
It's important to use the full width of the area. Going into neutral allows the rudders to keep steering and helps slow the boat so that when you engage astern the engine isn't fighting the momentum.

4 **Engage astern** Now put the throttle astern but without moving the helm, just use tick over to start with but add a couple of revs to get the prop walk and prop offset to start dragging the stern back round to port.

5 **Don't bottle it** Use astern for far longer than feels natural. You need to drag the bow right the way through the turn otherwise the moment you go ahead again the boat will go back to where you started.

6 **Complete the turn** Once the 180-degree turn is complete, engage ahead gently so that the movement astern is halted, then as the boat moves forward, unwind the full starboard lock as you regain steerage.

how to
BERTH A TWIN-ENGINED BOAT USING ONLY ONE ENGINE

On pages 112–115 we tackled how to turn a twin-engined boat if you lose one of the engines, and now we're looking at how to berth it safely, too.

A nice large space is always welcome, however, if the only available ones are smaller or you want to try to get it back on your home berth then it's advisable to run through this procedure before you need to do it for real.

Generally, it's easier to berth on the opposite side to the working engine, so if your starboard engine is working, aim to berth port side to. As usual, the elements also play a major part and the wind blowing you on to the berth might seem like the easiest option. However, with only one engine working, your steerage options are limited. If you don't get it right first time then your chances of getting away again for a second attempt are dramatically reduced. That's why I prefer to aim for a berth where the wind is blowing the boat off the berth as it gives you more control over your approach speed.

On page 113 I explained why using the rudders to turn the boat in the opposite direction to the way in which the one working engine wants to push it gives you the best chance of completing the turn. Now that same skill will allow you to position the boat with much greater control than just allowing the wind to berth the boat.

Having worked out which berth you are going to attempt, the first step is to get the boat nicely balanced against the elements, with the working engine furthest from the pontoon. This will allow you to make a controlled approach, although you may find you need to keep the speed and momentum slightly higher than on your normal berthing routine in order to maintain steerage. If you are

choosing a blown-off berth then this slightly higher speed is offset by using a steeper angle of approach. This means that if you do misjudge your speed slightly, a burst of power astern will not only slow the boat but, being the engine furthest away from the pontoon, will straighten it up, too.

The technique in our images works well with twin shafts, outdrives and even IPS drives, which actually steer

remarkably well with only one engine, but you have to use greater anticipation and a lot of helm. Having a bow thruster and even a stern thruster as well will make it easier, but don't rely on them; practise using just the engine and helm as you will learn a lot about how well balanced – or not – your craft is by using the elements and controls to best effect. With a bit of practice, you should even be able to do it single-handed.

1 The preparation
Fender the boat well and try to find a berth that you can approach into the elements. Take a fairly coarse angle of approach that keeps the working engine (starboard in this instance) on the outside and use the rudders to overpower its natural inclination to turn to port.

2 The approach
With the boat nicely balanced against the elements, and using nudges of ahead on the working outside engine with starboard helm to counteract its natural bias to port, you should be able to hold a steady line as you approach, allowing the crew to lasso a cleat with the bow line.

3 Getting a line on With the bow lassoed, remove most of the slack from the bow line and make it fast. Now either gently engage astern or let the elements move the boat astern until the line becomes taut.

4 Tucking in
Once the line is taut leave the working outside engine in astern so that the prop walk and offset from the centre line gradually pull the stern of the boat in towards the pontoon. You won't need to move the wheel.

5 Making contact
Leave the engine in astern until you almost touch the pontoon. That continuous tension will keep the boat walking towards it. If you go into neutral too early the boat will move away again.

6 Attach the stern line
Just before you touch, go into neutral for a moment to cushion the contact with the pontoon, then back into astern to hold the boat firmly alongside. You can now step off and attach the stern line.

how to
MOVE A BOAT SIDEWAYS

Being able to move your boat sideways is an essential skill for getting out of tight spots. Of course, some new boats now have the option of a joystick that does the hard work for you but it should be possible to replicate this manually with a bit of practice. Some techniques work better on outdrives while others work better on shafts, so you'll need to try them on your own boat to see what works for you.

The idea is to alternate between moving the bow and stern in little steps so that it gradually creeps sideways in a crabbing motion. A good bow thruster helps enormously but even without one, you should be able to achieve it.

In a twin sterndrive boat moored starboard side to, the technique is to fender the starboard bow, apply full starboard helm, then click ahead briefly on the port engine to push the bow in

towards the dock. This lifts the stern away from the dock, allowing you to straighten the helm and apply a click of astern on the port engine to lift the bow off without pushing the stern back in. You may need to repeat this a couple of times to come well clear of the dock before putting the helm to port and applying a click of starboard ahead to push the bow out further (keeping an eye on the stern to ensure it doesn't move too close to the dock), then keeping the helm to port and applying starboard astern to move the back end further out. On shafts, the technique is much the same but some craft respond better to use of the helm than others.

Realistically, most new craft over 9m (30ft) long (and therefore most twin-engined shaftdrive boats) are likely to have a bow thruster as well and where fitted, it would be foolish not to use it. The Sessa Marine 43 we used for the photographs was on sterndrives but did have a bow thruster fitted. When using a bow thruster, it is imperative to remember that the stern will move in the opposite direction as well, so in our starboard side berth, a good burst of bow thruster to port moves the stern to starboard. As the bow comes away, either use port ahead or starboard astern to move the stern to port and away from the dock.

With practice, it's possible to use both bow thruster and engine controls together to literally walk the boat sideways. Nearly all twin-engined boats will turn on the spot with one engine ahead and one astern, so if you thrust against the ahead engine, you should be able to move the boat sideways with only very little movement fore or aft.

1 **Moving the stern out** In order to get the stern out without creeping forwards, fender the bow area well, then put the helm to starboard and engage port ahead. This pushes the bow against the dock and lifts the stern clear of the pontoon with minimal forward movement.

2 **Moving the bow out** Now that the stern is well away from the dock, centre the helm and engage port astern to lift the bow away, too. Repeat steps one and two for a second time to keep the boat moving sideways and ease it further away from the dock without moving forwards.

3 **Straightening up** Once you've created enough of a gap between the stern and the dock, drive the bow further across, using helm to port and starboard ahead, then straighten up the boat with the same helm and starboard astern to keep the boat moving sideways.

4 Using a bow thruster To achieve the same manoeuvre using a bow thruster, give it a good burst of thrust to port to push the bow off the dock, then turn the wheel to starboard and use the port engine ahead to drive the stern clear and walk the boat sideways.

5 All at once Once you are confident with the above method, you can do it all at once by thrusting to port with the helm to starboard and port ahead so that the boat crabs away from the dock in a single motion. If there's something close ahead, you can achieve the same result with port helm and starboard astern.

6 Using a Joystick If you're lucky enough to have a joystick fitted, you simply push the joystick to the side and let the computer juggle the throttles and helm for you. However, even then, it rarely moves the boat parallel, so a small twist is usually required to keep it travelling in the right direction.

how to
FERRY GLIDE

Ferry gliding is the art of using the flow of water or wind past your boat to move it sideways across that flow. Traditionally used by ferries to cross fast-flowing rivers, it's also extremely useful for leisure craft when arriving at or leaving a tide or wind-affected berth. It works by using your boat's steering and power in combination with the wind and water to create a sideways force.

It's best to do this with the bow into the elements, as the shape of the bow makes it easier to see and feel the effect. Before you attempt it, look carefully for any obstructions upstream, such as moored vessels, bridge stanchions or posts, which may deflect the flow and make things less predictable. For this photo shoot we had a nice downstream flow on the river and very little wind, so I positioned the bow upstream and slowed to a stop, judging when we were stationary by using a transit on the barge – our target. To prevent us being swept downstream, I applied a click of ahead every few seconds to counter the current.

I then turned the helm towards the target and engaged ahead momentarily to point the bow to starboard, so that the flow of water started pushing on the port side of the boat.

The aim is to prevent the boat from moving forwards or backwards, while allowing the water to move the boat sideways. You should carefully monitor the angle of the boat towards the target – the steeper the angle, the quicker the boat will move sideways. If you find yourself moving sideways too fast, reduce the angle by bringing the helm away from the target, in this case by turning to port and using a click of ahead.

If you want to come alongside your target, wait until you are within 1m (3.3ft)

of it before bringing the bow parallel to it as the target may well be generating its own turbulence that tries to push you off again. This will allow you to come alongside nice and gently. As you touch, put the upstream line on first to act as a brake.

To leave, angle the bow away from the target – the water flow over the rudder or outdrive alone may be enough to start the sideways motion. If not, use one click ahead to get the motion started. Remember that the stern quarter will be pushed in towards the pontoon and may need an extra fender for protection.

Positioning yourself stern to the elements works just as well but requires more practice as the blunter shape means the sideways motion can go from gentle to quite fast with only a small change of angle.

If you are using the wind rather than the water as your source of sideways motion, it's the same manoeuvre but it will be your boat's windage rather than its underwater profile that affects the speed of movement and again may need more practice.

What about wind and current? Simply adjust your initial start position so it's balanced against both elements. Remember that the wind may be influenced by the object you are coming alongside too so be prepared for last-minute changes in direction.

The key with ferry gliding is that the slower you make your boat go sideways, the more control you have and the gentler you will come alongside. It's a great skill to master that looks effortless, uses very little power and really shows a skipper's appreciation of the elements.

1 Balancing the boat

Point the bow into the current/flow and position the boat parallel to the target (in this case, the barge). Check it's not moving fore or aft by lining up a transit on the barge using occasional clicks of ahead to keep it stationary.

2 Starting the ferry glide

With the boat now facing upstream, turn the wheel towards the target and engage one short click of ahead to get the whole boat angled towards the target so that the water starts to push on the upstream side (in this case, the port side).

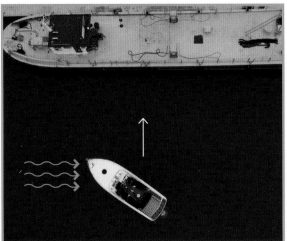

3 Approaching the target

As the boat starts moving sideways, you may need the odd extra click of ahead to prevent it from being swept backwards. Turn the wheel to port to slow your speed of approach to the target.

4 Leaving the target Turn the wheel away and engage ahead for one click to point the bow out into the stream and let the flow of water work its magic. Watch your stern as this will also push it closer to the barge.

5 Control your speed Now that more water is flowing on to the starboard side of the boat than the port, the boat will start to move sideways. Increase the angle to go faster or reduce it to slow down.

6 Stern first You can carry out the same manoeuvre with the stern pointing into the elements using clicks of astern to stop you from moving forwards. Remember, though, that the blunter stern will be less precise than the bow.

how to
USE PROP WALK TO YOUR ADVANTAGE

When the propeller on a boat is turned by the engine, the majority of the force it produces pushes the boat ahead or astern. However, the shape of the blades also creates a small amount of sideways force, which creates a turning effect on the boat as well. This force has several names – prop walk, propeller effect, transverse thrust – they all mean the same thing but for clarity I will call it 'prop walk'.

It's most apparent and easiest to see on a shaft-driven boat. You can visualise it by mentally replacing the propeller on your boat with a paddle wheel while viewing it from astern; when the propeller is turning clockwise, so to the right (called a right-handed propeller), it wants to paddle the stern of the boat over to starboard. When moving ahead, this also causes the boat to pivot by turning the bow to port. When moving astern, the effect is much more pronounced as the wash from the propeller is no longer going over the rudder so you can lose steering. Now the turning effect of that same right-handed propeller in astern is to push the stern to port – and hence the bow to starboard. All of this happens the other way round with a left-handed propeller that spins anti-clockwise in ahead.

Knowing the rotation of your propeller is fundamental to all manoeuvres carried out on a single shaftdrive boat, especially when going astern. Using this force to help with tight turns rather than hinder them is crucial as it gives you the ability to turn the craft 'short' – using the least amount of room.

To find out which way your boat's propeller turns, while still securely tied to the berth briefly engage astern and see which side of the boat the wash comes out. If it exits to starboard, it's a right-handed propeller, if it exits to port then it's a left-handed propeller.

Having worked out which way it turns and knowing that its effect is much greater in astern than ahead, it makes sense to always turn the boat using the prop walk effect in astern to push the stern the way it naturally wants to go and balance any fore and aft motion by using ahead and the power of water flowing over the rudder in short bursts to keep the turn going.

On a twin shaftdrive boat, the starboard engine will usually have a right-hand propeller and the port engine a left-hand one. When both are used ahead or astern at the same time their prop effects cancel each other out but when used individually the prop walk of each engine can actually aid the manoeuvring process.

1 Identify prop type

Work out which way your propeller turns either by watching the shaft when you engage ahead or by seeing which side of the boat the wash exits when put it in astern. This one spins to the right so in astern it will walk the boat to port.

2 Think ahead

Tight turns require careful planning in a single-engined shaftdrive boat. Knowing this boat wants to turn to port in astern, I have entered the space to port of centre so I can start the turn by steering the bow hard to starboard.

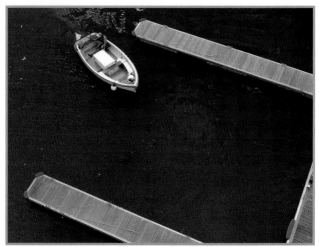

3 Start the turn

Move the rudder hard over to starboard and use a burst of ahead to initiate the turn. Use as much room as you can but don't get too close to the pontoon as the stern will be swinging to port around its natural pivot.

4 Going astern

Now put the engine into astern using the power of the prop walk to continue the spin. You do NOT need to change the position of the rudder because the wash is going under the boat, rendering the rudder temporarily redundant.

5 Keep going

Stay in astern and keep spinning around. Allow the boat to gain some momentum by using some of the room astern. Now if you need more turning space or to overcome any wind and tide, you can repeat steps 3 and 4 until you have enough clearance to exit the space.

6 Complete the turn

Now the turn is complete, you can go back into ahead. Think carefully where the stern is though as you may need to steer gently to port as you go ahead to ensure the stern moves away from the pontoon as you exit.

how to
DRIVE TO WINDWARD

Making passage to windward is what good planing motor boats are all about. The ability to travel at 16 knots or more into the wind is one of the great party tricks our sailing counterparts envy. Choosing the right moment weather wise is the key – more wind means it's getting lumpier for those aboard – and the style and design of your hull will play a vital role in how much wind you can cope with. In a boat of less than 12.2m (40ft), a wind strength of up to F4 is perfect passage-making weather.

If you have a tidal element in your cruising area, any tidal movement against the wind will amplify the waves and can make a passage that would be relatively pleasant in non-tidal areas a real challenge. Wind and tide together generally makes it no worse than a non-tidal area.

Planing boats are at their most efficient either when cruising slower than their displacement hull speed, roughly 5–8 knots depending on length, or when fully planing at 16–18 knots or more. Speeds between these two ranges (8–15 knots) tend to use a lot of fuel for a relatively small gain in speed, but if trimmed correctly, can make for a more comfortable passage in lumpy weather.

So, having chosen your passage timing and the weather that comes with it, how do you get the best out of your boat when travelling upwind? First, you need to get the boat up to speed. Shaftdrives and pods don't usually have any means of trimming the drives themselves so you'll need to use the trim tabs/blades to make any adjustments. Sterndrives and outboards do have adjustable trim angles so when heading into the wind, trim the outdrive legs all the way into the hull, usually about -5. Then, apply enough power to get the boat past its 'hump' speed, at which point it will start to plane on the surface of the water, rather like skimming a stone.

Some older, heavier or underpowered craft will also need an application of trim

tabs to assist with getting the boat on to the plane. By adjusting the trim tabs down, the water pressure acting against the lowered tabs lifts the stern up and pushes the bow down. This can help the boat to plane earlier, or stay on the plane at slower cruising speeds.

Once the boat is on the plane, you can use the tabs to adjust the running attitude to suit the conditions (see opposite for details). This can make a significant difference to comfort and speed. You can also use them to dial out any leaning caused by uneven weight distribution or a stiff crosswind.

1 **When ready to plane** head straight upwind at tickover with the helm in the centre position. If the boat has sterndrives or outboard engines, pull the legs into the fully down, tucked-in position. Now push the throttles positively ahead until you feel the boat start to rise on to the plane.

2 **Watch the speed** on both the log and GPS and once above your planing speed (around 16 knots), ease the throttles just enough to stop accelerating and let the boat settle. Now you need to assess whether the trim angle is correctly set for the conditions, or if the boat needs trimming fore or aft.

3 **The trim tabs are best used initially** as a pair to adjust fore and aft trim. This will drop the tabs/ blades into the water to raise the stern and drop the bow. Beware that on some installations, the tab controls may be cross-wired.

4 If the trim tabs are down too far – like here – you will physically see the bow lower and the washline (where the boat enters the water) moving forwards. On many boats, the speed will also drop and the steering will become heavier. These are all indications of too much boat in the water, so trim up.

5 Conversely, if the bow is too high, as in this photo, then the boat is effectively dragging the stern, which will compromise the view forwards from the lower helm and make for a lumpier upwind ride by allowing the waves to hit the flatter aft sections of the hull rather than the deeper vee of the bow.

6 Now the lateral trim can be adjusted. Here, our boat is leaning to starboard, so we need more starboard trim tab down to generate extra lift on that part of the stern and raise the starboard side up.

how to
HELM DOWNWIND

The design of the latest generation of hulls, along with the power-to-weight ratio of modern diesels, means most planing motor boats are astonishingly capable at travelling downwind in quite rough conditions. The large, flared bow means you can drive them on to the rear face of each wave and hold it there until the weight pushes through and you can move on to the back of the next one.

Be aware that if the wind has been blowing in the same direction for more than a few hours, the waves generated can be moving at considerable speed. Travelling in the same direction as the wind, it's also very easy to miss a gradual increase in wind speed and you can suddenly find that it's got very rough!

If this is the case, you need to consider how your vessel will handle the conditions if it becomes too rough to continue at planing speeds. If you have to slow to displacement speed, or if a problem means you need to turn back, reaching the nearest port might require a long upwind slog.

Skippers of craft that have a displacement or semi-displacement hull form need to be particularly cautious, especially if they have a wide, square stern, as this makes them more susceptible to being picked up by a large following wave. If the stern is picked up and the boat starts to surf, this may cause the bow to be driven into the trough of the wave ahead, slewing the boat around.

To counter this, displacement and semi-displacement craft generally have larger rudders so the skipper needs to be ready to change the boat's heading as soon as they feel the stern being lifted.

Driving a planing boat downwind is relatively simple and usually involves maintaining a straight course while applying enough power to get the boat riding up and over the waves. Even when tempted by flatter seas, don't travel at more than 2/3 throttle so that you have enough power in reserve to outrun any larger waves that do catch you.

1 **To get your boat on the plane** going downwind, look for a flatter piece of water, especially if conditions are rough, and make sure the helm is pointing straight ahead. Then throttle up until the boat is comfortably on the plane.

2 **Now throttle back** to a comfy cruise until your speed is slightly faster than that of the waves. Try to avoid using the trim tabs and keep the bow high so that you can use the mid-section of the hull to break and flatten the waves.

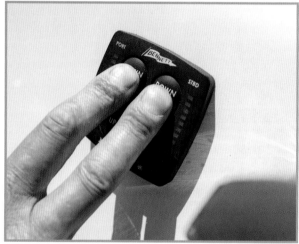

3 **Here, the boat can be seen rising** over each wave with the bow trimmed as high as it will go. The waves are slightly on the quarter rather than dead downwind, which produces a better illustration of the wave shapes in this photo.

4 **The key to going downwind** is to keep the bow high so that it cannot be tripped up by any larger waves catching you up. This picture shows just how far down the hull you want the spray to be exiting.

5 **Don't be tempted to travel at full speed**; 2/3 throttle is a sensible maximum that always leaves some in reserve so that you have power to open up and outrun a wave breaking right behind you.

6 **In a bigger downwind sea**, the skipper should be using the throttle all the time to power up to and ease over each successive wave, making good progress while keeping the craft safe.

how to
DRIVE IN A BEAM SEA

We have looked at helming a motor boat windward (pages 132–135), where we use the trim tabs to bring the bow down and allow its shape to cut the waves, and downwind (pages 136–139), where we raise the tabs to keep the bow up and rest the hull on the back of the waves. Now let's look at travelling in a beam sea, when we can make excellent progress if we concentrate on keeping the boat trimmed relatively level.

The issue with a beam sea or beam wind is that it's trying to push the boat downwind and off course. Your natural instinct is to counteract this effect by steering into the elements and reducing the leeway. This will cause the boat to lean into the waves, making for a harder ride and a more tiring passage. It also changes where you need to look, as you have to keep one eye on where you're going and one eye on the waves rolling into you.

In this situation, using the trim tabs to level the boat also makes helming much easier. This involves lowering the tab on the windward side to create lift and

counteract the lean induced by steering into the breeze. Levelling the boat allows the hull's vee to cut through the waves for a softer ride and lifts the topsides higher off the water for a drier passage and better vision. The trim tab also gives a gentle steering effect by increasing drag and pivoting the boat to windward, exactly where you want it to go. If the wind picks up more, you may want to overextend the windward tab to induce a slight lean away from the waves. It helps the waves slide under the boat rather than slamming into the beam.

If the wind is slightly forwards of the beam, maybe tab down a bit on both sides to get the bow cutting through the chop before adding tab on the windward side to level the boat. If the wind is coming from slightly behind the beam, you usually just need some windward tab, but all craft are different so experimentation may be needed.

As the sea state worsens, you'll need to lift your vision to look at the waves further ahead and pick a path around the largest ones. This involves deciding early if you want to turn to windward to go behind a larger wave, turn slightly downwind to run just ahead of a breaking wave or turn fully downwind as a wave breaks right ahead of you. Trimmed correctly, your boat will be safer and more responsive, allowing you to enjoy the ride.

1 Leaning into the wind We have set off on passage towards our destination but a wind on the starboard beam means our efforts to stay on our heading by steering towards the breeze are causing the boat to lean into the wind.

2 Assessing the situation From the helm position, the lean is even more apparent. It makes it difficult to hold the correct course, waves slam against the hull, spray comes into the boat and the passage is more tiring for skipper and crew.

3 Correcting the lean Apply the starboard tab to lift the windward side of the boat and level the attitude. The hull is now running level for a softer, drier, less tiring ride. Applying the right amount of tab is a process of trial and error to find the correct balance.

4 Running level Now the boat is level, you can see how much less spray is being thrown out from the bow. It can help coming 20 degrees downwind of your destination's heading to get the boat level before working your way back to the correct heading.

5 Leaning away from the wind This time we've applied a little bit of extra tab to induce a slight lean away from the waves. As the wind picks up, this can help the bigger waves to slide down the side of the hull rather than slamming into you.

6 Enjoying a drier ride From the helm, the change is subtle, but the feel of the boat will be a good deal softer. The added advantage is that the ride will be drier, as any spray tends to land further aft.

how to
THROTTLE AND TRIM YOUR ENGINE

Knowing how to throttle and trim a planing boat correctly is a key skill, especially for owners of smaller, faster craft like RIBs and sportsboats. The first thing to sort is your driving position. At speed, the relationship between the wheel and throttles becomes crucial and it's imperative, especially in smaller boats, to keep control of them even when being bounced about. Your seating position is vital, too: you need to be stable but relaxed so that you don't accidentally

move the controls. Lastly, the single most important item to have to hand is the kill cord, which needs to be attached as soon as the engine is running.

When speeding up, the actions required are similar in any sea direction.

What does differ is how you trim the engine and any trim tabs fitted to the boat. The first step is to have a good look round to ensure it's clear, then with the helm straight, the engine trim in the fully down position and the tabs up, engage ahead at tickover. Now progressively push the throttle forwards so that the boat starts to increase speed. As the bow rises, add more throttle until you are fully planing. You don't need to go that fast – many craft will plane at 15–16 knots. I find 20 knots a safe, sensible speed to practise at.

When at a steady planing speed, trim the engine up slightly, usually for around two seconds – you will hear it, see it on the trim gauge and the tacho will show the revs rise a small amount and the speed increase. This is because lifting the bow means there is less boat in the water and therefore less drag.

If you are running into the waves, you may want to reduce the trim to keep the bow down so that the sharper forward part of the hull is cutting through the chop rather than slamming into the waves with the flatter aft section. If you have trim tabs fitted, these can also be lowered to raise the stern and push the bow down even more. An easy way to remember this is: upwind, bow down.

Conversely when going downwind, you want the bow up and out of the water so you don't stuff it into the back of the next wave as you overtake the previous one.

Trim the engine up and lift the tabs; don't lift it too high, though, as this may cause the boat to porpoise. This time, the phrase to remember is: downwind, bow up.

To slow down, check there are no boats coming up fast behind you, then trim the engine back down as you bring the throttle back towards tick over.

Keep it progressive, though – if you slow too quickly your stern wave may catch you up and flood the transom. Once the stern wave has dissipated, go back into neutral.

1 **Check the kill cord** As well as sensible kit and a good-quality lifejacket, make sure the kill cord is attached and working by pulling it off the kill switch to check that the engine stops. Try to fit it so that you don't pull it out accidentally (round your thigh is usually a good option) and check there is a spare aboard in case you fall out of the boat.

2 **Practice makes perfect** Try using the trim on your engine before you get under way so that you can get a feel for it and see how quickly it moves up and down. You need to know where the trim switch is by instinct and practising will help you to add just the right amount when needed without having to take your eyes off the helm.

3 **Hand position** I like to rest the heel of my hand on top of the throttle body so that it acts as a stable pivot point even when I'm navigating through rough seas. I then flex my wrist to apply more or less throttle, leaving my thumb free to adjust the trim.

4 Coming on to the plane

Make sure the wheel is straight and the engine is trimmed down, then steadily apply more throttle until the bow lifts up and over its own bow wave. Note how much boat is in the water as I accelerate.

5 Trimming upwind

When running into the waves, it helps to keep the bow trimmed down enough to keep a small conection with the water so the deepest part of the vee can cut through the waves either by reducing the engine trim or lowering the tabs to push the bow down.

6 Trimming downwind

When running with the waves you want to trim the engines higher to keep the bow out of the water so the boat's initial contact is further aft. This will help prevent stuffing the bow when you overtake one wave and land on the back of the next one.

how to
MAKE FAST TURNS SAFELY

Driving a fast boat safely will always involve making turns, either pre-planned ones to reach your destination or when avoiding other craft, debris or waves. Practising turning the boat at speed so that you know how much helm, throttle and trim to use before it starts to skip sideways is crucial to avoid endangering yourself, your crew and your vessel.

The key to a safe high-speed turn is a smooth co-ordination of hands, throttle, trim and vision to minimise changes in the balance and attitude of the boat. A sudden decrease in power will pitch the weight forwards, pushing the bow deeper and raising the stern, increasing the chance of losing grip at the stern. Conversely, a sudden increase in power will raise the bow and lower the stern. Turning with any sudden change of direction will increase the angle of heel. This change in speed and lateral g-force will further test the hull's ability to maintain its grip on the water and the heel will bring the propeller(s) closer to the surface, making it easier for them to suck in air. This aeration when turning can also trigger hull slide.

Ultimately, if you are heavy-handed with the controls, you are more likely to induce hull slip or even a 'hook', when the stern loses all grip, the bow digs in and the whole boat pivots rapidly and violently around it with dramatic and sometimes dangerous results.

The ability to turn the boat smoothly and consistently is key to maintaining speed and safety. I break this down into three steps. First: look. You should be keeping a good lookout at all times anyway but before turning you need to look intently, not just at where you are going but at the water you intend to turn on to. Is it clear of other boats and debris? Is it flat with no breaking waves or peaks that could upset the boat? Most importantly: do not just look at the bow; look and steer where you want to go. The boat will follow.

Second, trim. The boat/engine needs to be trimmed down a bit from where it was before the turn. If you're running upwind, you may already have it trimmed down so it could just need a small adjustment. However, if you're heading downwind or in flat conditions with the engine trimmed up then you will need

to trim it down enough to increase the propeller's bite.

Finally, throttle. It's good practice to ease the throttle before you execute the turn, though not by much as this risks upsetting the balance, do it just enough to let the bow settle. Now turn the helm with a steady motion. Any turn slows the boat, so as you turn, gently increase the throttle so that you are maintaining a steady bow angle. Too much throttle and the bow will rise, too little and it will fall. Lastly, as you start to exit the turn and straighten the wheel, add more throttle to lift the bow and accelerate away.

1 Preparing to turn Make sure the boat is properly trimmed and settled before attempting any turns. Note that I am sitting with my body relaxed and my hands on both the wheel and the throttle.

2 Looking round Before making any turn, have a really good look all around you to check for other boats and ensure that the water you are turning towards is clear of debris and any large waves that could unsettle your turn.

3 Trimming down Bring down the trim to increase the wetted surface of the boat and the propeller's bite, both of which will reduce side slip. I've also moved my hand position on the wheel to prepare for turning to port.

4 Throttling back Ease the throttle a touch prior to commencing the turn. This will give the boat a chance to settle and ensure you have some power in reserve to maintain speed through the turn and accelerate out of it.

5 Steering Turn the wheel steadily and consistently in one smooth movement, then progressively but gently increase power to give positive drive through the turn while keeping the bow level.

6 Exiting the turn Look at where you want to go, rather than at the sea in front of the bow. As you straighten the helm, power up to lift the bow and trim up to keep the engines transmitting power efficiently into the water.

how to
DRIVE IN ROUGH WATER

Rough weather takes practice, a fair amount of getting it wrong and sometimes a very wet boat and clothing. Make no mistake, the person who has never got it wrong off a wave has never been out on a really rough day!

The skill comes from knowing what to do and by reading the waves well ahead of the one you are on – not easy if you can barely see over the next one.

There are a couple of simple steps to follow. First, think about the boat's trim angle as it encounters each wave – if the bow is dropping then add a touch more power to lift it. Likewise, if the bow is rising then consider easing the power so you don't fly off the top of it. Second, never travel too fast because at some point you may need more power to lift the bow and if there is no throttle left it can go horribly wrong.

The direction of travel also affects how you deal with the waves. Waves tend to be less intimidating downwind when you are riding on the backs of them rather than climbing the faces. The technique here is to sit on the back of the wave, letting the wave's speed dictate your progress, then, as it starts to dissipate, power up to drive on to the back of the next one. However, it can also be the most risky. Go too late and the breaking crest of the wave can cause you to lose drive as the propeller struggles for grip in the frothy white foam, leaving you to get swamped by the next breaker. Go too early and you risk punching through the wave with spectacular results but a very wet boat. In both cases, you may need to ease the power just enough to regain drive.

Upwind is generally hardest. Here, you need to drive every wave as an individual crest – the key is to avoid shooting off the top and landing heavily in the trough beyond. Generally, the larger the wave, the deeper the trough behind it, so it's

crucial to ease the power before the top so that you lose momentum as you come over the crest. Then, as the bow starts to drop, power up again to lift it ready for the next one.

Beam seas can offer the best opportunity to make good progress by

picking your way through the flatter water between each wave set. The key is looking upwind to see what's coming then deciding how to deal with each wave. The first option is to turn upwind and ease over the crest. The second is to turn slightly downwind to outrun it, then come back on to your course. The final option is to ease the power and let the wave pass in front of you.

With practice, it's possible to make good progress in all three conditions. However, the defining factor will always be the capabilities of your boat and crew.

1 **Downwind trough** Having eased over the crest we are now at the bottom of the trough, ready to power up in order to lift the bow and climb on to the back of the next wave.

2 **Downwind crest** The power is on and the bow has risen to rest on the back of the next wave. As that dissipates, get ready to ease over the crest and continue.

3 **Upwind face** Running upwind, you need power to raise the bow and climb up the face of the wave but be ready to ease the throttles just before the top so you don't shoot off the top.

4 Upwind crest As you come over the wave, shut the throttle right down so you don't drive off the wave, then get ready to power back up the moment you land in order to lift the bow for the next one.

5 Upwind trough This was a deeper trough and heavier landing than expected, but I've already put the power back on so the bow is rising for the next one.

6 Beam sea Picking my way across the waves, I am always looking at least two or three waves ahead to windward, so I can spot any bigger ones and choose my plan of action.

how to
DRIVE AN IPS BOAT BETTER

When IPS drives arrived back in 2005, they were viewed with a degree of scepticism by many people, including me. The joystick technology may have been very clever, but it seemed like a complicated way to solve the issue of how to drive a boat well.

Many years on and IPS has become the standard drive system for many craft in the 12–18m (40–60ft) bracket, partly because it's more fuel efficient than shafts and frees up space for accommodation, and partly because it helps convince potential buyers they can drive a bigger boat. But while it has solved much of the angst associated with tricky berthing manoeuvres, it doesn't always encourage good seamanship.

So how do you use IPS effectively? The theory is simplicity itself: twist the joystick and the boat will rotate, push it in any direction and the boat will move that way too. So where's the problem?

Well, having spent the summer watching countless IPS boats churn their way around the marina with excessive amounts of noise, wash and rocking, it seems that some owners aren't finding it quite as simple as it sounds. And with ever larger boats starting to use IPS, the problem is only going to get worse. However, with a bit of guidance the whole process can be made much smoother and less stressful.

The first thing to appreciate is that the controls may be simple but they are also very sensitive and linked to very powerful engines. When you release the joystick, although the drive stops instantly, the boat's momentum does not. This is exacerbated when you ask the boat to do two different things at once, such as moving sideways whilst also twisting. The two competing sets of messages send the pods into overdrive, creating large amounts of wash and lots of rocking.

This is where the seamanship part comes in. The trick is to slow everything down by bringing the boat to a halt, using transits ahead and to the side to gauge when it's fully stationary, before commencing any manoeuvre. As soon as it is, the IPS 'hold station' function really comes into its own, although that too has its issues as it can disguise how much wind and tide there is by fighting the elements when sometimes it would be better to let them assist you.

In summary, rather than putting all your faith in IPS's ability to muscle its way out of any situation, you're usually better off bringing the boat to a halt, assessing the situation and using your own skill and judgement to take advantage of the elements and the IPS drives to execute a slower, gentler manoeuvre. On pages 206–209 we look at how to master berthing an IPS boat.

1 Stopping your boat

As with any tricky manoeuvre, it pays to bring your boat to a complete stop at the start point of your approach by balancing it against the elements. Make sure your boat is stationary by using transits both ahead and to the side to check it has stopped moving.

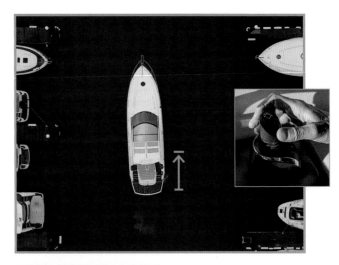

2 Moving forwards

Push the joystick forwards to engage both drives ahead. To stop the forward movement, you will need to pull back on the joystick; simply letting go of it will put the drives in neutral but won't stop the boat's momentum. Practise doing this as gently and precisely as possible.

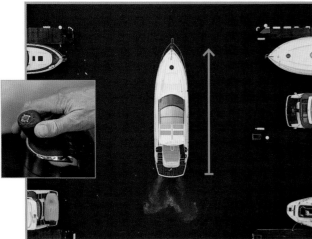

3 Moving sideways

Pushing the joystick to the side you wish to move towards is easy, but because the bow usually moves slower than the stern, you may need to correct this with a slight twist to keep the boat straight.

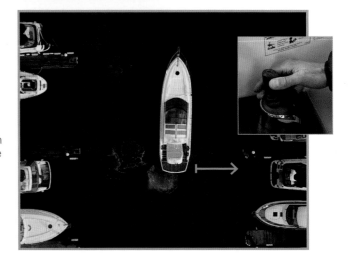

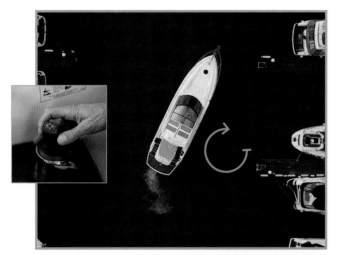

4 Turning on the spot
Twist the joystick and practise stopping the rotation so that the boat is pointing where you want it to be. Judging the momentum to use the minimum of counter twist is the goal.

5 Moving diagonally
Getting the boat to move diagonally is a tricky one as you need to get the right balance of side and ahead. Early IPS boats struggled with this but with a bit of practice, newer ones will do it.

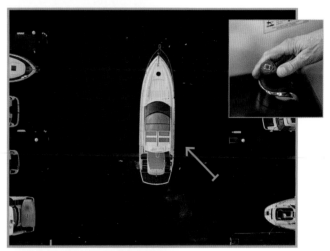

6 Avoid overdriving
This is easily done due to the power of the drives. If you're not acutely aware of the building momentum, you can easily overdrive the boat and then have a heart-stopping moment bringing it to a halt.

berthing

how to

how to
LEAVE A DOCK

Leaving an alongside berth, especially on a smaller boat, can just be a case of pushing the boat far enough out to allow you to drive away. It's usually easiest to push the bow out as it's lighter and moves quicker than the stern. When leaving in forward gear, be careful not to steer away from the dock too soon or the stern may swing in and hit the pontoon. Any additional wind or current will either help or hinder you. If these are pushing you away from the berth, it should be possible to just let go and let the elements take the boat away. However, if they are pushing you back on to the berth and making it much trickier to leave, what should you do?

If possible, you should try to leave into the elements, as this gives the most control and allows the slowest departure. So, if the elements are on the stern, then it's best to leave stern first. The shape of the bow helps here as there is already a small gap between the point of the bow and the dock, which it can pivot into as you steer the stern away from the dock. In light conditions, this may allow you to simply apply full steering lock away from the dock and engage astern.

If the conditions are a bit stronger, then you can increase the angle of departure by putting the bow closer to the dock before departing. To do this, first make sure there is a fender to lean on, then apply full helm towards the dock before engaging a brief click of ahead gear, then immediately back into neutral. Now apply full lock away from the dock and engage astern gear. This drags the boat away at a wider angle and enables a good, positive departure from the dock.

If the elements are on the bow, then in light conditions you might get away with one of the two stern first techniques described above but, ideally, you want to leave bow first into the elements. This poses two problems. First, many small boats don't have a bow thruster to help push the bow away from the dock. Second, the stern is often square, difficult to fender and easy to damage on the dock. So, if there is no bow thruster, the best way to get the bow out is to use a stern spring.

Rig a line leading forwards from the boat's stern cleat to a cleat on the dock at least 1m (3.3ft) ahead of it. Loop it around the cleat and then take it back aboard, preferably to the same cleat you started from.

Only use as much line as you need – too long and it might snag when trying to release it – and fender the stern well, even on a RIB, as the tube will be pushed against the dock, making it vulnerable to damage from sharp protrusions.

Now engage astern so that the line goes taut and levers the bow away from the dock. As soon as the bow is out as far as you need it to be, engage neutral, slip the line, bringing it all inboard smartly, and then drive ahead, once again keeping a close eye on the stern's proximity to the pontoon.

1 Leaving ahead On a small boat, the easiest way to leave is to position yourself towards the front of the boat and push the bow away from the dock then engage ahead, steering gently away from the dock.

2 Watch the stern Having pushed the bow away from the dock, be very careful not to turn away from the dock too hard or too early as the pivoting action of the boat means you risk clipping the dock with the stern.

3 Leaving in astern Turn the wheel fully away from the dock and engage astern. This will drag the stern away and create room for the bow to pivot towards the dock without hitting it. Take care in onshore breezes.

4 Creating more angle

If you need a bigger angle due to an onshore breeze or a boat astern of you, then turn the wheel fully towards the dock and use a brief click ahead to drive the bow in and bring the stern out.

5 Pulling away

Having pushed the bow in and created the extra angle, go into neutral, then turn the helm fully away from the dock and engage astern. This will pull the boat off the dock, even in a strong breeze.

6 Using a stern spring

Fender the stern, then rig a line from the stern cleat to the dock and back. Turn the helm towards the dock and go gently astern. When the bow is clear, engage neutral, slip the line and motor away.

how to
BERTH IN WINDY CONDITIONS

Berthing on a windy day can be one of boating's most stressful tasks, particularly if the wind is attempting to blow your boat away from your intended berth. On page 101 we covered how to balance your boat against the elements in order to hold it steady. Now try combining this with deliberately driving the boat to windward to assist with the berthing manoeuvre.

When it's windy, unless the boat is balanced bow or stern to the elements, you will only have a small window to work with before the wind puts you in a boat-damaging situation. On the day we shot these photos, we had a steady 18–20 knots of breeze across our intended berth with gusts of up to 25 knots.

To demonstrate how you can use the boat's weight and momentum to counteract the wind and buy you the time to execute the manoeuvre before the wind starts to push the bow around, we deliberately used the bow thruster only when absolutely essential. Of course, in real life you should use it when you feel the need but bear in mind that electric bow thrusters only have limited power and run time, so try not to rely on it too much. The objective is to use the wind as a decelerator of the boat's movement towards the berth rather than accelerating it away from it.

To do this effectively, you need a start position that allows you to approach your intended berth from a downwind position. This may mean going past your intended berth and turning the boat round to give you the required approach. In a dead-end aisle, this will require some positive boat handling to ensure you don't get swept downwind and into further danger. The way to do this is to drive past the berth, bring it to a complete stop by balancing the stern against the wind, then start to reverse the boat upwind towards your intended berth before beginning any turn.

The technique will work on most boats but we used a twin outdrive boat that had plenty off windage, a very light bow and a modest bow thruster to ensure it was suitably challenging. Twin shafts usually offer better grip on the water and tend to be fitted to heavier craft so should prove easier to manoeuvre. Pod drives and/or joystick controls will make the process easier but still require the same planning and approach as they commonly have a slower reaction time. Bow and stern thrusters (when fitted) can save a lot of stress but relying on them without considering where you will end up if the wind overwhelms them is a risky strategy.

As with all berthing manoeuvres, make sure you've fendered the boat appropriately. That means fenders on both sides at the correct heights so that if you do get it wrong, all you need to do is stop the boat moving fore or aft; most fenders will cope with drifting sideways into something but if you compound the problem by trying to power against them, you're much more likely to cause damage.

1 Approach with the wind on the stern Drive past the berth if necessary then using a transit abeam, bring the boat to a complete stop and balance it against the wind. This is your starting position for the final approach before you begin reversing towards the berth.

Wind is blowing across the berth

2 Reverse towards the berth Reverse positively into the wind from your balanced position in order to gain some momentum before executing the turn into the berth. The wind will slow your approach and keep your speed as low as possible while still enabling you to maintain steerage.

3 Drive the stern into the berth Keep driving into the berth using the boat's momentum to carry you towards the pontoon before the wind has a chance to blow you off it. In this photograph you can still just see the turn from the wash on the water. Make sure your crewman is ready with the stern line.

4 Tuck the stern in Here, I'm using the port throttle astern to slow the swing and drive the stern into the berth. Make sure you keep watching the bow to catch it with the thruster or a click ahead if it starts to get blown downwind. You need the stern close enough for the line to go on easily.

5 Get the stern line on first This applies whether you berth stern first or bow first and makes things that bit easier. Once the stern line is secure, either hold the bow with the thruster or a click ahead on the outside engine to keep the bow positioned for the crew to tie up.

Wind is trying to blow the bow off

6 How to go in bow first If you have no option but to go in bow first, you need to aim for the very far end of the berth. Keep driving ahead to maintain momentum, then use the outside engine astern to slow you and take the stern towards the dock, making it easier for the crew.

how to
LEAVE A WINDY BERTH

Trying to leave a berth in a controlled manner with a stiff crosswind can be daunting – especially if it's a tight berth and your neighbour's boat is shinier and more expensive than yours!

If the wind is pinning your boat against the pontoon, it makes it hard to leave before you get pushed back on. Conversely, if the wind is blowing you off, the issue is how to escape before you get blown into your neighbour. Positivity is the key to avoid a fender-bashing session but don't confuse positivity with speed. Crew play a big part as well, and setting the boat up with easy-to-slip lines so they can remove them and bring them inboard exactly when asked really helps.

As always, the first step is to assess what the wind and tide are doing. I like to think of this as 'look up' (at the wind) and 'look down' (at the tide) – remember that you need the wind information for the surface of the water, not just the wind at yacht top and flag level.

If being blown on, the boat won't move much whilst the lines are removed but try to arrange your lines so that the last one can be released from on board. If you're

berthed stern in, the first step is to get the bow away from the pontoon. This can be with the bow thruster (if fitted) or a stern spring to force it out. Once the bow is out, select ahead with the outside engine to move the stern away from the pontoon, then alternate engines or use both ahead whilst steering out of the berth.

If moored bow in, then ease the stern away with the inside engine in astern, then as it moves out, use both engines astern to back out positively. If it's really windy, you may need to use the outside engine ahead and the inside engine astern while stationary against the pontoon to help twist the stern out.

If the boat is being blown off the berth, that you need the same positivity because the moment you remove the bow line, the bow will start to blow away. You may be able to control this with a bow thruster but if in doubt, use a slip bow line and pull against it with an engine astern, or use a short stern line and drive ahead against it. This forces the boat on to the pontoon until you're ready to manoeuvre. To do this effectively, you need to rig the lines on short, simple slips so when you go into neutral, the boat will lift off the pontoon, allowing the lines to be pulled smartly in while you drive positively out.

1 Exiting a berth in a crosswind

Moored stern in and with a stiff wind blowing you off the pontoon, you will need to exit the berth swiftly before being blown on to the neighbouring boat. The crew needs to release the bow line first and then come swiftly back aboard.

2 Releasing the bow line

The crew has released the bow line and quickly placed it back on board before moving to the stern. If it's really blowing, it may be easier to rig a slipline so that the crew can release it and bring it back on board while standing on the bow.

3 Using a bow thruster

A burst of starboard thrust helps control the bow while the crew walks to the stern, releases the stern line and boards. Now exit positively with the downwind engine first before you get blown on to the neighbouring boat.

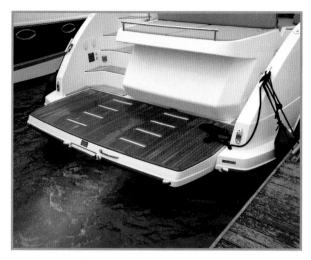

4 Using a stern line

Here, the close proximity of the blue boat and a stiff breeze blowing your boat towards it means you need to leave in a positive but controlled manner. A bow thruster would help but you can achieve the same result using your lines and engines instead.

5 Pinning the boat against the pontoon

The solution is to rig a short, quick-release stern line then use the port engine ahead to pin the boat against the pontoon while the crew removes all the other lines, ready to leave.

6 Releasing the stern line

With the other lines removed, drop the engine into neutral. This makes the stern line go slack, allowing you to release it and the bow to drift out. Put the outside engine ahead to control the bow and leave.

how to
BERTH SINGLE-HANDED

Boating alone can be a glorious experience. Obviously you need to approach it with a safety-first mindset, but I really enjoy time alone on the boat, and the satisfaction that comes from dealing with all the challenges is immense.

Inevitably it's leaving or arriving at a berth that presents the biggest challenge, even though it's really just an extension of the normal crewed process with some additional planning and preparation to ensure it goes smoothly. One of the most common concerns is arriving back at your original berth to find that the perfect conditions you enjoyed on your departure have changed and you are now faced with a much more difficult, if not near-impossible challenge. The answer is to change your plans and choose a berth that you can manage. And never be embarrassed to ask the marina or a fellow boater to take your lines.

As with so many aspects of boating, preparation is key. Leaving a berth efficiently is done by assessing the elements, which line comes off first, and how to get the boat clear. I usually start at the bow by removing the bow line and walking aft, coiling it as I go so it can be neatly stowed away. Then I remove the stern line, step smartly aboard, go to the helm and leave in a positive manner before I'm blown back on to the berth.

I like to make it easy to remove the lines and fenders by stopping the boat with the stern to any elements so the bow doesn't get pushed around. I then tidy them away on deck without rushing. I always try to do a couple at a time and then return to the helm to check my position.

When arriving somewhere new, I find doing a drive-by of my intended berth allows me to check its suitability and assess the wind and tide. Unless the conditions are really light then a berth where the elements are assisting you on to the pontoon will generally make things easier. Fenders will need to be set and adjusted to the correct height, and I always lay the bow line along the side

deck (taking care to pass it up and over the bow rails) so it can be picked up easily as soon as you step ashore. I leave the stern line loosely flaked and attached for the same reason.

The key is not to rush. It sounds obvious, but many a berthing manoeuvre is ruined by rushing in, especially since you have no crew to shout out the distances as you make your approach.

Aim to get the whole boat into the berth and stopped before you attempt to step away from the helm, leaving the elements to close the last few inches to the pontoon. Judging distance is crucial – stop too far away and the elements may push you on too fast; get too close and you risk not stopping in time. In both cases, you are likely to bounce off the fenders and get pushed back out of the berth.

Only when you're certain you've judged it correctly should you leave the helm and walk to the exit point to get your first line on. I tend to go with the stern line first, then walk forwards, taking the bow line with me. The exception is when I am berthing into a strong tide or wind. In that instance, stepping off at the stern and taking the bow line forwards first may be more practical to prevent the boat moving aft.

1 Release the bow line

With the wind holding you gently on, release the bow spring and bow line, taking care to throw the first part on to the foredeck before walking aft, coiling the line as you go so you can place the remainder on the side deck or pull it through the rails.

2 Release the stern line

Having made your way aft, undo the stern line, then step aboard with the line before making your way to the helm in preparation for leaving. You should already have a mental plan of how you are going to leave the pontoon so take it calmly and don't rush.

3 Leaving the pontoon

Use the bow thruster to push the bow away from the pontoon, then use the inside engine astern to reverse out positively so that you get clear before the wind has a chance to blow the bow back on.

4 Arriving at a berth

Bring the boat to a halt and balance it stern to the wind. This allows you to leave the helm and put out two fenders at a time, returning to the helm to rebalance the boat before adding the next pair. Bring the bow line down the side deck so you can easily step ashore with it.

5 Entering the berth

Drive positively up to the far end of the berth, then stop it a foot from the dock so the wind pushes it the last few inches. This allows you to get to the bathing platform before it bounces back.

6 Securing the boat

Once you're certain the boat has stopped, move to the stern and step off with the lines in your hand. Attach the stern line first, then walk the bow line forwards and tie it off.

how to
LEAVE A BERTH SOLO

Crew are a great help to have on a boat but being able to use your vessel single-handed also has its advantages. It's especially useful when teaching new crew what to do as they can watch the first time, help out the second time and do it all themselves from then on. Single-handing also has some important safety considerations as it makes you realise what can be accomplished alone and what is just too difficult or dangerous.

Leaving an alongside berth single-handed on an 18m (60ft) craft takes planning and requires using the boat's controls and the prevailing conditions to your advantage. The boat we're using has twin shafts and a bow thruster, and we are starboard side-to with a gentle breeze holding us on. There is also an ebb tide on the stern.

The first step is always to work out what will happen and how. If I undid all the lines at once, initially the boat

wouldn't move with the wind but as the ebb tide edged it forwards along the berth, the breeze would then pivot us around the end of the pontoon, and both the wind and the tide would continue to push it across on to the other boats. So, with the dangers established – the corner of our own berth and the boats opposite – how should we leave?

Before you do anything, first check that the engines are running, the gears engage and the bow thruster is working. Next, take the springs off so that there is only a bow and a stern line holding you in place. A quick glance should confirm that

the bow line is reasonably slack, while the stern line is taut from the ebb flow. Also check that the fenders are correctly positioned as you will need to move the bow away from the pontoon, which will push the stern in towards the pontoon.

Once satisfied, remove the bow line first and lay it along the side deck as you walk back towards the stern in case you need to put it back on at short notice. With this sorted, prepare to remove the stern line. I like to pull the taut part of the line slightly to reduce the tension before starting to undo and coil the excess line from the cleat. Now release the last loop that is securing the boat either from the boat itself or the pontoon and step onboard, making your way swiftly to the controls. Next, check that the boat hasn't already started moving along the pontoon. If it has, a small click of the pontoon side engine astern will stop that movement and bring the stern slightly away. Then, use the bow thruster for long enough to push the bow well away from the pontoon. This also pushes the stern closer, so to prevent it getting too close you will need to use the outside engine ahead. This will pivot the boat and move the stern clear.

As the boat comes clear and roughly parallel to the pontoon, either use both engines ahead for half a second to gain some momentum or alternatively each engine in turn to walk the boat out of the berth. I generally keep the helm straight ahead for this movement. The next key point is to stop the boat mid-aisle so that you don't turn with any momentum and get swept on to the boats opposite. In this instance, we need to turn to starboard to leave so either use both engines astern to stop or just starboard astern so that you are not only slowing but starting the turn for your exit. I like to use a transit to my side to check that I am turning on the spot with no down-element drift. The turn can be accomplished either by using one engine at a time or one ahead and one astern to make the turn more positive. I use the helm for the turn on the ahead engine. Always aim slightly up-element as you finish the turn so that you are heading towards the safe side for your exit.

1 **Ready to leave** Engines on, controls checked – the bow line should be off and laid back on to the side deck so that it's easy to pick up again if you need to re-berth in a hurry.

2 **Remove the stern line** I like to pull the stern line in just a fraction before removing it as that gives me a bit of slack to work with. It also brings the stern closer to make stepping onboard easier.

3 **Thrust the bow out** As soon as you reach the controls, use the bow thruster to push the bow slowly away from the pontoon. As the bow moves out, the stern will be pushed in against the stern fenders.

4 Pulling away

Apply the outside engine ahead (in this case, the port one). This not only lifts the stern away from the pontoon but also straightens the boat up parallel with the pontoon. Now use both ahead for half a second to clear the berth.

5 Start the turn

Use starboard astern to slow the boat and initiate the turn. As the boat comes to a standstill, use helm to starboard and port engine ahead while using a side transit to ensure the boat isn't creeping forwards.

6 Exit the aisle

Slightly over-rotate the turn so the bow ends up heading towards the safer up-element side. Finally, exit nice and slowly, in full control.

how to
BACK INTO A BERTH IN A SINGLE-ENGINED BOAT

The first choice to make when arriving at a berth in a single-engine boat is whether to go in bow or stern first. Going bow-in is usually simpler, however, best practice is to leave the boat as you found it, which in this case was stern-in.

As a stiff wind is blowing across the aisle in this example, there are two crucial points to get right to avoid hitting the boats downwind. The first is the turn into the aisle, as that tailwind will increase any momentum carried into the turn. The second is knowing when to turn downwind before entering the berth. Both manoeuvres will take you towards the craft on the other side of the aisle, so the key things to focus on are:
• using the helm and gears positively to balance the boat against the elements before making either manoeuvre;
• keeping over to the windward side prior to making both manouevres;
• leaving the final turn until the bow is level with the centre of the berth.

Many skippers fail to realise how much momentum the boat gathers from the elements alone. They go into neutral on the approach to the aisle but then neglect to check how fast they are still moving. This means that their turn into the aisle is accompanied by a slide towards danger. The key is to fully stop the boat using astern gear and transits to check you're not moving. To make the turn itself, use helm hard to port and ahead to drive into the aisle. Keep going all the way round until your bow is on the windward side of the aisle then slowly crab along at an angle with your bow pointing slightly upwind.

As the bow passes your berth, turn to starboard so it ends up on the downwind side just past the berth. Go as close as you dare to the boats on the other side of the aisle but make sure you leave enough room to stop. This also brings the stern to port and closer to the berth. Now put the wheel to port and the engine astern to bring the stern up to windward and towards the berth. Use enough astern and wheel so that you end up balanced stern to the wind. If you have a bow thruster you can use small bursts to keep

the bow where you need it – don't use long bursts as that will skew the stern the other way and cause more problems.

Now using clicks of astern and wheel to suit, move the boat in small steps back into its berth. When fully in, kill any astern motion with a click of ahead. Put the stern line on first to stop any forward motion before securing the rest.

If you find the boat gets blown off before you can get the bow line on, return to the helm and engage ahead with the helm straight. This will bring the bow in and hold the boat nicely against the pontoon. Too much helm towards the pontoon forces the stern out and makes getting back off harder. Once the bow line is on, go into neutral and add the springs.

1 Turning into the aisle First, bring your boat to a complete stop by going into astern before you attempt the turn (note the direction of my boat's wash). Failure to do so risks the combined effect of the wind and your momentum carrying you into the boats on the downwind side of the aisle.

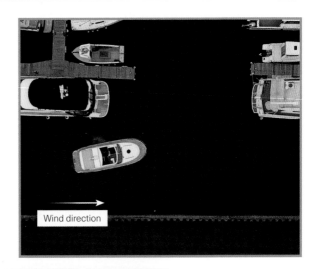

Wind direction

2 Completing the turn Push the bow all the way through the turn and back up to the safe windward side of the aisle. You can then crab your way slowly along the aisle at this angle in order to prevent your bow from being blown downwind and back towards danger.

3 Correct positioning As the bow passes your berth, put the wheel to starboard and click into ahead to push the bow as close as you dare to the boats opposite on the downwind side.

4 Room for error

As you edge closer to the boats on the downwind side of the aisle, make sure that you leave enough room to stop any forward momentum. Here, I have just used wheel to port and astern to stop the boat.

5 Backing into the berth

Using clicks of astern and wheel to port or starboard, get your stern nicely lined up with the berth. Once in position, use small clicks of astern to reverse slowly into the berth.

6 Securing the boat

Get the stern line on first to stop the wind blowing you forwards. Once it's on, use ahead with the wheel straight, which will push the bow in and hold it alongside while you add the other lines.

COME ALONGSIDE IN A SINGLE-ENGINED BOAT

Coming alongside in a single-engined boat without a bow thruster can be one of the more difficult skills to master, especially on your own. If you're new to the boat I'd always recommend establishing how many turns there are lock-to-lock on the steering before you try any manoeuvres, then centring the helm and briefly engaging ahead and astern at idle. That way, you'll know where the engine is directing its thrust and how much the boat moves when you use a single click of gear engagement in either direction.

For this demonstration, we used a single- engined 7.5m (24ft) RIB, which behaves like any other small sportsboat, and two pontoons to practise on – a large hammerhead with an offshore wind to contend with and a mid-river pontoon affected by wind and tide. The key here is that the angle of approach is not governed by a set number of degrees but by when you are able to balance the boat against the conditions using minimal steering or throttle inputs – this is your 'start' position. You can now govern your approach speed using clicks of ahead, neutral and the boat's natural momentum to bring you gently alongside.

Approaching the pontoon

When berthing bow to the elements, as you close the pontoon, turn the wheel away from the dock and use a click of ahead to take the bow away from the pontoon while still maintaining enough momentum for the boat to carry on drifting towards it. Once the bow has started to move away, go into neutral and turn the helm towards the pontoon so that when you engage astern to stop the forward momentum, it will also bring the stern in gently against the pontoon. Ideally, you will end up perfectly parallel and stopped alongside. If your stern ends up touching first, then you need less lock towards the pontoon; conversely, if the bow touches first, you need more lock towards it. Neither of these is a big problem provided you have ensured the boat has come to a complete stop rather than impacting the pontoon while still moving ahead or astern. Fenders will help with any accidental contact but there is only so much impact they can absorb.

If you find yourself approaching downwind and downtide, then you have two choices: either carry on past the pontoon then turn around so that you are coming in bow to the elements or moor stern to the elements by reversing back towards the pontoon. This requires extra caution as the square stern means that it's harder to get alongside. In this situation, it's often easier to put the stern line on before it touches the pontoon, make it fast and then use a click of ahead with the wheel towards the pontoon to bring the boat alongside.

If single-handed, a mid-ship line is a good way to hold the boat alongside while you sort out lines. The key is to get that balanced start position nailed.

1 Finding balance

The 'start' position is crucial. This is where the boat will remain stationary bow into the elements with minimal helm and throttle inputs. From this position, I can use clicks of ahead to close the pontoon.

2 Drive the bow out

Turn the helm away from the dock and use a click of ahead to drive the bow out. With practice, you will learn how to create just enough momentum to reach the berth without actually hitting it.

3 Bring the stern in

Reverse the helm so that you're steering towards the berth. Now engage astern for long enough to bring the stern against the pontoon while halting forward momentum so that the boat stops parallel.

4

Approaching stern first
This time, we are starting with the boat stern to the elements but also balanced in the 'start' position. Use helm to move towards the dock and astern gear to bring the stern closer to the pontoon.

5

Straightening up When berthing stern first, turn the helm away from the dock and use a click of astern to stop the stern hitting the pontoon, but with enough momentum to keep moving. A stern fender is vital here.

6

Stopping alongside
Use one click of ahead to stop the boat parallel and alongside. Secure with a line. I am using a mid-ship line first to hold me alongside, giving me time to then add a secure bow and stern line.

how to
BACK INTO A BERTH

Backing into a berth is rapidly becoming an essential skill for motor boat owners. In the Mediterranean, almost all berths are arranged for stern-to mooring and even in the UK the height of many modern craft makes it impossible to get on or off anywhere other than the bathing platform.

It's not really that different to entering a berth bow first, however, the shift of pivot point and more restricted view astern can make it harder to master. The same principles apply: go as slowly as you can whilst still maintaining control and get the boat balanced on the wind and tide as you approach, so that if the manoeuvre is not going to plan you can simply stop and start again.

I like to get a view of the whole berth before entering it, even if that entails going past it and then turning around before berthing. With a twin shaftdrive boat I always centre the helm and use alternate engines to back in slowly but with an outdrive boat I also use small wheel movements so as not to give the bow any scope for getting out of shape.

The most important point to remember when moving astern is that the boat's pivot point shifts aft from its usual position when helming in ahead to a new position roughly a third of the way in from the stern. This means that the bow will move twice as far in the opposite direction to the stern. For example, when trying to back in towards a floating

pontoon on your port side, engaging the starboard engine astern will pull the stern of the boat towards the pontoon but it will also swing the bow out to starboard and towards any neighbouring boat.

Most of us find berthing easier when the wind is blowing us on to the berth, so on a light wind day it makes sense to start with the wind blowing the bow towards the berth and control its drift downwind either by being positive when driving into the berth and/or using the bow thruster (if fitted). On a windier day, I would always start from a downwind position and use the momentum of the boat towards the wind to overcome it rather than risk being blown in too quickly.

You will need to be positive and use the bow thruster to stop the bow from swinging too far upwind, rather than fighting the wind whilst trying to bring the bow back under control. Spotting the crosswind and knowing how it's likely to affect your bow allows you to make a better judgement about which side to approach from.

The hardest berthing manoeuvre is when the wind is bang on the bow. A stern-to berth and a decent breeze on the bow can be a real challenge. Lastly, any tidal movement needs to be taken into account, as whilst concentrating on the stern of the boat, the tide can catch you out. In our images, the tide is flowing strongly towards the stern end of the pontoon, which has helped steady the boat for me in the same way that a strong breeze on the stern would.

1 Check the berth
Before attempting to enter the berth, drive past it to get a closer look and check the effects of wind and tide (inset) before swinging away and positioning yourself in the right spot from which to start the manoeuvre.

2 Line up the stern
Having observed the berth, swing the bow away to present the stern to the berth. In this instance, we are aiming for a port side-to berth. The key is to ensure you have full control of the bow before reversing in.

3 Move astern
With the boat central to the berth, begin moving astern, starting with the starboard engine but using alternate engines and checking the bow to ensure it doesn't stray too far over to starboard.

4 Control of the bow If the bow strays too far away from the pontoon use a burst of bow thruster to keep it in check. In this instance, a gentle breeze is exacerbating the situation by pushing the bow out.

5 Look both ways It's important to monitor progress astern and at the bow. Here, I have engaged port astern to move the stern away from the pontoon and bring the bow back towards it.

6 Set your lines Get your stern line on first then add the bow line to keep the bow against the pontoon. The tide is on our stern so I'll need to add springs to stop us from being pushed forwards out of the berth.

how to
DOCK A SINGLE SHAFTDRIVE BOAT

On page 128 we looked at how to identify and use prop walk to turn around in a tight space. Now we're going to learn how to use that same prop walk to help dock a single shaftdrive boat. The launch in these photos has a right-handed prop, which pushes the stern to port when going astern, so all things being equal, mooring port side to is going to be easier. That's because when you use astern to slow the boat as you approach the berth, it will naturally pull the stern in towards the dock.

The speed and angle of your approach will depend on what the wind and tide are doing. If you are docking into the elements you will need to use a moderate angle and a little bit more speed before using astern to stop the forward movement and kick the stern in. If you are docking with the elements then you will need to use a slightly steeper angle of approach but a slower speed, then slightly more astern to stop and drag the stern to port on the prop walk The same theory applies to a boat with a left-handed prop, except your preferred berthing will now be starboard side to.

It is perfectly possible to berth a right-handed prop boat starboard side to or vice versa if the wind and tide are strong enough to make this an easier option – you just need to go as slowly as possible and use a much shallower angle of approach so when you go into astern to slow the boat it doesn't move the stern too far away from the dock. You should aim to end up with the boat almost alongside but needing a touch of ahead with full port rudder to bring it past parallel (slightly bow out), then use a last click of astern that pulls the stern out, the bow in, and stops you – all in one go.

Having used prop walk to get your single shaftdrive boat into a berth, you now need to work out how to leave the berth while overcoming it. Leaving in

astern will be tricky as the prop will want to push the stern back towards the dock, so ahead is usually easier. In ahead, the prop will still want to turn the bow towards the dock but not as quickly. The key is to get the bow as far away from the pontoon as possible and generate some forward motion to gain steerage before the prop walk has a chance to push the bow back in.

There are several ways to achieve this. I am not a great fan of pushing the bow

out by hand but there are occasions on a small boat when this is the simplest option. I call this the 'manual bow thruster' and it is best done from the boat rather than the dock, so use a foot or a boat hook to steadily push away from the pontoon.

Another option is to use a trick that I've seen on inland waterways, which involves lifting the stern fender out and pulling on the stern line. This helps force the bow out and allows you to motor away while keeping an eye on the stern.

The last method is to use a stern spring. Ensure the stern is well fendered, then take the stern line forwards and loop it around a dockside cleat then back to the stern cleat. Now engage astern against this spring and force the bow out. When you're happy with the angle, go into neutral, slip the spring line and motor away, being mindful of the stern and not turning too early.

1 The approach

If your boat has a right-handed propeller, docking port side to is the best option. With the boat moving slowly towards the dock, engage astern to halt movement and let the propeller walk the stern in.

2 Attach the stern line

Once the boat has stopped moving forwards, drop the engine into neutral and let the stern carry on sliding gently in towards the pontoon, so you can place the line over the cleat.

3 Leaving the dock:

option 1 A push-off is often the quickest solution in a small craft but always do it from the boat rather than the pontoon and be certain that you are balanced before you push!

4 Leaving the dock:

option 2 While the boat is stationary, lift the stern fender and pull on the stern line. This will make the boat pivot on the starboard quarter and force the bow out from the pontoon allowing you to leave in ahead.

5 Leaving the dock:

option 3 Set up a spring by leading a line forwards from the boat's stern cleat around a pontoon cleat and back to the same stern cleat. Using a ball fender to take the pressure, engage astern and force the bow out.

6 Pulling away

When the bow is far enough away from the dock, go into neutral, slip the stern spring and pull it back on board before going ahead. Keep an eye on the stern to ensure that it doesn't clip the dock.

how to
USE A BOW THRUSTER EFFECTIVELY

Bow thrusters have become standard equipment on most craft over 9m (30ft) and even some smaller ones offer them as an option. Almost any craft will benefit from having one and it's certainly the one extra I would always tick on a new boat (and consider retrofitting to an older boat), especially if I were purchasing a single-engined craft or one with high windage.

We all know the basics of how to use a bow thruster, but overuse and/or poor usage often mean that skippers can cause themselves as many problems as they solve. I like to consider the bow thruster as an extra crew member who can lend a hand when needed but shouldn't automatically be relied upon.

Electric bow thrusters have a finite period of time they can run before excess heat or power draw shuts them down. If you need to use it for that long, the chances are you are attempting the wrong manoeuvre. Some even come with a hold facility, but treat it with caution – it's a hold for a few moments, not indefinitely. Hydraulic ones are able to run for longer periods and can be used to hold the craft in position whilst lines are attached.

All bow thrusters are simple to use – just push the switch or lever in the direction you want the bow to go and it will follow – but there are a couple of things to watch. They really only work effectively when the boat has stopped or is moving at less than a knot – more than that and the water is moving past the thruster's tunnel too quickly for it to be effective.

The next thing to remember is that the thruster might well be moving the bow to port or starboard but the pivot point roughly in the centre of the craft means that the stern will be going in the opposite direction. So if your crew is trying to attach a stern line and you keep thrusting the bow towards the pontoon, you are almost certainly driving the stern out and making it harder for them.

I always advise using a short burst, then a slight pause, then a second burst and even a third if needed. These short bursts are often more effective than one long one and prevent overdriving the bow, which would mean you having to stop that momentum by driving it back in the other direction. Pauses between bursts also allow the propeller and motor to stop so that if you need to change direction you aren't putting excessive strain on the system. Be careful not to overdo the number of bursts, though – if the wind does take the bow, many thrusters won't be powerful enough to drive it back upwind. Far better to know when you're fighting a losing battle and use the engines to move off safely and start the manoeuvre again.

A good exercise when berthing is to drive the bow slightly too close to the pontoon and use the thruster to push it away from the dock, helping to tuck in the stern and making it easier for the crew to attach a stern line.

Stern thrusters work in much the same way as bow thrusters, but as they tend to be fitted deeper below the waterline, they are often quieter, which means that skippers commonly hold them on too long with exactly the same pivot issues as the bow thruster.

To recap, use small bursts, pause between each one and don't forget to monitor movement at the other end of the boat as well.

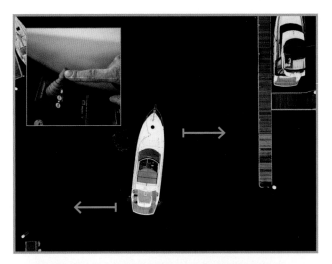

1 Beware the pivot point

Pushing the bow thruster lever to starboard drives the bow closer to the pontoon, but because the boat pivots around a central point, the stern is also moving away from the pontoon, which can make life tricky for crew trying to get a stern line ashore.

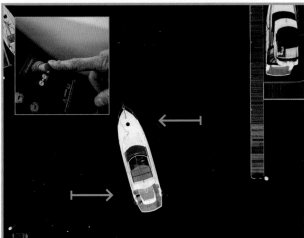

2 Watch the stern

This shows the boat in the same position but after a few short bursts of bow thruster to port. The bow is now moving nicely to port but you can see how far the stern is being driven to starboard as well, which could cause it to hit the pontoon when leaving a berth.

3 Leaving a berth

Using the thruster to push the bow away from the dock makes leaving easy but you need to monitor the stern, too. Make sure the stern quarters and bathing platform are well fendered.

4 Use the outer engine

Once the bow has been thrust far enough out, use the engine furthest from the dock first. This will also bring the stern clear before going ahead on both engines.

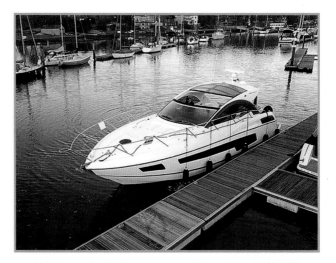

5 Coming alongside

Aim a fraction too close with the bow and then thrust the bow away just before you come to a halt. This helps the stern to come in closer and makes it easier for the crew to get a line ashore.

6 Bringing the bow in

Once the stern line is on, thrust the bow back towards the dock for the crew to attach a bow line. A small burst should be enough, but you can keep adding bursts if the breeze demands it.

how to
LEAVE A BERTH IN A SINGLE-ENGINED BOAT

Single-engined craft are making a comeback, boosted by lower prices, reduced servicing costs and better fuel economy. However, manoeuvring a single-engined craft takes practice. On the plus side it does simplify the question of which engine to use!

The Marex 310 Sun Cruiser we borrowed has a single Volvo D6 sterndrive. It also has a bow thruster, so whilst it's possible to leave a berth without using it, it does make life easier.

There are three key points to remember when manoeuvring a single-engined boat:

1 Turn the wheel before engaging gear.
2 Use short bursts of ahead, astern and plenty of neutral so the boat never gains too much momentum – slow is pro!
3 Look and think ten seconds ahead to ensure each movement is planned rather than a panicky reaction.

In these photos there is a fresh breeze from the stern blowing us towards the boats on the other side of the aisle, and limited turning room.

Task one is to single up the lines by removing the springs; the breeze from astern means that you should remove the bow line first, then the stern line, so you can get to the helm before the wind blows you out of the berth.

With the helm straight, engage ahead, nudging in and out of gear to pull clear of the berth without gaining too much momentum. Now, depending on the wind strength you have two options. Either engage a brief dab of astern with the helm straight to bring the boat to a halt, then turn the wheel full to port before engaging astern again to pull you back towards the windward side of the aisle. Or, if you've already stopped drifting forwards, go straight to step two.

Now go back into neutral, turn the wheel full to starboard and go ahead so that you drive the bow round towards the windward side of the aisle. Depending on how well you've done the first part, you may be able to get round in one go but be careful, as the bow moves to starboard your stern will pivot to port, coming closer to the craft on the downwind side.

If your bow won't clear the boat opposite on the first attempt, go back to neutral, wheel to port and into astern again to create more room. Or if the bow goes round but your stern gets too close, go into neutral, wheel to port and ahead again to push your bow back downwind. Once both ends are clear, keep the bow high on the windward side and exit the aisle.

If you have a bow thruster you can use it to push the bow round more quickly. Again there are three points to remember when using one:

1 It works best when the boat is going very slowly or is stopped.
2 It pushes the stern the opposite way.
3 Use it in small bursts to avoid overheating the electric motor.

1 Casting off
Ensure the wheel is straight and the lines are singled up. With the wind on your stern port quarter, release the bow line first, then the stern line. Now nudge slowly ahead to clear the berth before the wind twists you.

2 Start the turn
Put the bow as close as you dare to the boats opposite, then use astern to bring it to a halt. Now whilst in neutral, turn the wheel hard over to port and go back into astern to pull your stern to port and bring the bow to starboard.

3 Backing up
Apply nudges of astern with the wheel still to port, using small gear engagements to avoid building up momentum and allowing you to use all the space behind you. The wind on your stern will slow you.

4 Bring the bow round

Now put the wheel hard to starboard and engage ahead to push the bow round towards the windward side of the aisle. If you have a bow thruster, using a burst to starboard will help the turn.

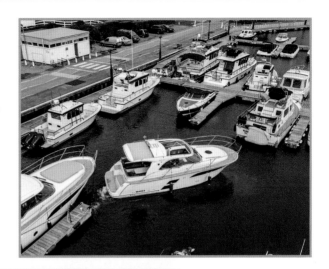

5 Watch your stern

If you have enough room, keep it in ahead and push the bow right round but don't forget to watch your stern quarter as it will pivot the other way and get closer to the boat opposite.

6 Exit the aisle

You can see just how much the boat has slid to port on the wind so keep this angle, with your wheel turned slightly to starboard, to push the bow to windward and exit the aisle safely.

how to
BERTH AN IPS BOAT

When berthing a conventional shaft or sterndrive boat, the simplest technique is to nudge the bow in at an appropriate angle and once it's close enough, tuck the stern in with a blip of astern as you bring the boat to a halt.

It is possible to use this technique on an IPS boat but it's not ideal as the pod drives find going diagonally relatively hard. I think it's easier to drive an IPS boat as if it were a castle on a chess board by moving a square at a time, either forwards, backwards or sideways. This plays to the IPS system's greatest strength and makes it easy for the helmsperson to use the joystick by pushing it in one of four directions without having to worry about twisting it at the same time.

On pages 156–159 we showed some simple IPS manoeuvring techniques. This time we will build on that so that you can join the manoeuvres together for smooth,

seamless berthing. The crucial part is the ability to reference exactly where the boat is in relation to the dangers. For this, I use a pair of transits ahead and to the side so that I can see exactly what is going on. This allows me to spin the boat on the spot regardless of wind and tide, using small corrections to stay safe, before continuing to drive the next part in a straight line.

The control given by the joystick allows you to be very precise but the power available also means that's its easy to overdrive, which then needs counter correction, creating lots of unnecessary noise, wash and discomfort.

You should aim to be as gentle and accurate as possible using small inputs to ensure you don't build up too much speed or momentum. This is especially important in stern-to mooring situations, where the wash from your pods risks stirring the 'lazy line' off the sea bed and flicking it around your props.

1 Positioning your boat

Don't enter the aisle until you are midway between the opposing pontoons and sure that any lateral drift has halted. Once you're certain you're not drifting sideways, move forwards so that the mid-point of your boat is central to the berth.

2 Preparing to enter

Stop the forward motion with a blip of astern and using your transits, twist the boat, repositioning against the elements as you go so that the boat stays nicely central. You can see our twist motion on the water's surface in this picture.

3 Line up the berth

Ensure that your boat is parallel to the dock but slightly away from the pontoon itself and half way towards the other boat. This takes practice as you naturally want to aim towards the pontoon.

4 Stop forward momentum

Once fully into the berth, use a gentle nudge astern to stop the forward movement, keeping the boat straight but slightly away from the dock until you are certain that you've stopped.

5 Moving sideways

Once stationary and correctly aligned, push sideways on the joystick and hold the boat alongside with gentle pressure to keep it in place while your crew attach the lines.

6 Leaving a berth

When leaving a berth, just push the joystick to the side but watch the bow so you can counter any tendency for it to lead. Here, a twist to starboard is required in order to keep it moving out parallel to the pontoon.

TIE UP A BIG BOAT

Whenever you are tying up any boat, small or large, you have to achieve the basic aim of securing it safely and making sure it will still be there when you return.

A wander around any marina will show a multitude of different ways of doing this, some neat and sensible, some less so!

Larger boats bring extra concerns when moving up from smaller craft. The 18m (60ft) vessel in this example weighs around 25 tonnes. That displacement together with the windage means that all the lines and fenders also have to be larger in size and weight.

Owners of craft up to 12m (40ft) generally use two lines to secure their boat, making sure the bow and stern lines are long enough to double up as springs. By the time your boat reaches 18m (60ft) I would recommend using at least four individual lines because doing so reduces the weight of each line and makes any adjustments simpler.

All berthing manoeuvres require the skipper to decide which line goes on first, where it is going to go and whether the crew steps ashore with it or lassoes a cleat from on board, followed by the next line and so on. Always double check that you have made your plan explicitly clear to the crew.

On larger craft, the height of the bow and the weight of the lines makes any form of lassoing from the bow pretty much a non-starter, so that generally means that the first line ashore will be a stern line. This can be set up either as a short lasso or a working end that the crew will step ashore with when called upon by the skipper.

Prepping the lines so you are ready before you arrive is key. I like to do this by walking the bow line forwards from the aft cockpit, with either a tied bowline or a spliced loop in hand, passing this over the top rail and on to the bow cleat from the outside to ensure it doesn't end up fouling the rails, then walking back towards the cockpit, making sure the line is lying neatly along the side deck. I then place the loose end on to the rail ready to be grasped by whoever steps ashore.

Next, I prepare the stern line so it is ready to be used either as a short lasso or an open end you can step ashore with. Once I have manoeuvred the boat into position and am certain it's stationary, I will, if alone, leave the helm, walk to the stern and lasso the stern line, making it fast before stepping ashore and walking forwards to pick up the bow line. As soon as these first two lines are secure, add an aft spring to stop the boat moving aft and

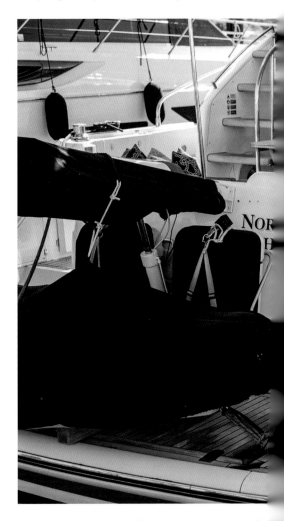

a fore spring to stop it moving forwards. Leaving some slack in the bow and stern lines allows for limited movement but try to keep the spring lines as long and taut as possible.

The size and positioning of cleats on many larger boats are often geared around Med-based berths where the craft all lie stern-to the dock. This often means that they are not best placed for an alongside berth. This can make it hard to use a long enough line for the stern without presenting a trip hazard. I combat this by using a cross line from an offside aft cleat to a shoreside point well behind the boat.

If you are expecting winds or a longer stay, reverse all the lines by taking the loop ends on to the dock so all the loose ends can be stowed on the boat. Also double up the bow line, using a second securing point, and add a cross line on the stern. Lastly, do your best to avoid short lines; in windy weather they will snatch and cause damage. If short lines are unavoidable, use rubber snubbers to give a degree of stretch.

1 Prepare your lines

Lead your bow line forwards, pass it over the rails and back on to the cleat. Lay the aft end on deck with the tail ready to be picked up from the shore and led forwards to the bow.

2 Stern line first

Once close enough, lasso the shore cleat with your pre-prepared stern line. Now secure it back on the boat, step ashore and walk forwards to collect the bow line.

3 Using springs

Once the bow and stern lines are ashore, rig fore and aft springs. Note how taut the springs are while the bow line is deliberately slack. A too-tight bow line means you can't pull the stern in.

4 Adding a cross line

A cross line is used to keep the stern in, allowing you to use a shorter, reasonably slack stern line that presents less of a trip hazard. This is also a good way of doubling up for longer stays or during storms.

5 Doubling up

I like to double up the bow line if I'm staying longer or if a spell of rougher weather is on the way. Try to use a second securing point. Note the loops/bow lines are on the dock cleats so that the excess line can be left on the boat rather than the pontoon.

6 Using a snubber

Too short a stern line will not allow the boat to move in choppy or rough weather, which will cause snatching and potential damage. A rubber snubber like this one enables a degree of stretch.

how to
RAFT UP TO ANOTHER BOAT

Rafting up to a stranger's boat on a busy visitors' berth is one of those moments that fills newcomers with trepidation. Not only is it a very public test of your boat-handling skills but you also know that whatever the outcome, you are going to spend the next few hours shackled in close proximity to the very person's boat you have just been using as a giant fender.

When done well, it can lead to an impromptu drinks party with your new rafting buddies. When done badly, it can make for a very frosty evening spent trying to avoid each other's gazes. The good news is that it's not hard to do, but it does require some preparation.

Your first step should be a drive-by, looking for a similar-sized motor boat to raft up to, simply because its shape and dimensions mean it's likely to be a better fit than a sailing yacht.

Having chosen your target boat, fender placement is crucial. This normally means setting the fenders at gunwale height, where the rubbing strake covers the join between the hull and superstructure. I aim to have 10cm (4in) of fender above the gunwale and the rest below, but take care not to position them over big hull windows, which may not be designed to take the weight. At the stern, I like to use a good-sized ball fender whilst coming alongside, before swapping it for something smaller once successfully berthed.

The berthing manoeuvre itself is made easier if your new neighbours are aboard to help with lines. If they aren't, then always try to berth against the wind or tide so that you can use them to control your speed as you come alongside. Once you touch, get the up-elements line on first so that you don't start slipping back. Try to do this from your boat so that if you need to pull away, you don't leave a crew member on the wrong boat.

Once you've got the upwind line attached then you can step on to your neighbour's boat and attach a line at the other end before adding springs to stop any further movement. It's quite normal to spend a good few moments adjusting the lines so that you can get on and off your neighbour's boat.

Traditional yachting etiquette says you should try to go over the foredeck when stepping on to your neighbour's boat but in practice, modern boats with large bathing platforms mean that most people are happy for you to cross from stern to stern.

Finally, once secure with springs on, it's helpful to rig a pair of long lines to the shore so that your neighbour isn't taking the full weight of your boat. They need to be tight enough to be doing something but not so tight that they are pinning your neighbour to the shore in a vice-like squeeze.

Leaving is a reversal of the process, making sure your last line is a slipline that can be released from your own boat before working your way out parallel to the raft.

1 Prepping your boat

Rafting allows two or more craft to moor alongside one another when there are no empty berth spaces left. First, drive by any potential rafting spots looking for a boat of similar style and size before setting your fenders at the correct height and preparing all of your lines.

2 Holding station

Once everything is ready, line up your boat parallel to the target boat using the wind and tide to slow your movement. In this case, the elements are on the stern off our boat. Plan to become stationary about 2m (6.5ft) off. This will allow you to control the situation as you make your final approach.

3 Final approach

As the wind is on our stern, I have angled the boat to ensure our stern touches first, enabling the crew to get a stern line on first. Your crew needs to do this without leaving the boat in case you need to abort and try again. Note the large ball fender protecting the bathing platform.

4 Attach your lines Get the upwind/uptide line on first, in this case a stern line, so it can start to take the weight of the boat as the wind and tide try to carry it forwards. Now you can attach the bow line (inset) so that the craft is secure before adding the springs to prevent any further movement.

5 Shorelines It's important to add shorelines in order to take the weight off the raft. In the main image, you can see that our shoreline is slack so the stern line of the boat inside us is taking the full weight of our boat and theirs. As soon as our shoreline is tightened (inset), the inside boat's stern line relaxes.

6 Preparing to leave Remove your shorelines and springs, then make any weight-bearing lines into sliplines that you can remove without having to leave your boat. When all is ready, slip the remaining lines and leave at a shallow angle that will take you safely away from the raft.

USE PILE MOORINGS

Pile moorings are relatively rare these days but it's important to know how to use them in places where there is no other option. In non-tidal areas, posts are fitted with a metal hoop to tie to, but in tidal areas the posts have a riser bar with a hoop that slides up and down to prevent lines chafing.

If there is already a boat between the piles, rig your fenders at rafting height, come gently alongside, then ease back and forth using their lines to place your own lines through the hoops. If you are the first to arrive at the pile, you will need to do this unaided.

There are a couple of ways of doing this but in both cases you will need to balance the boat against the elements so that you can make a controlled approach. First, arrange two free-running bow and stern lines that are long enough to thread the first one through one of the mooring hoops, then either drop back or go forwards so that you can thread the other one through the opposite pile's hoop.

If you're approaching both posts in line, motor slowly past the first one, close enough for your crew to thread the stern line through the riser bar and loop it back on board. Then, start paying out the line as you head towards the second post and repeat the process with your bow line. This technique works well for craft with good directional stability and practised crew. However, if the helm can't easily see the stern and crew, you can end up in a bit of a mess. That's why I usually find it easier to nudge the bow towards the up-elements post first, then let the wind or tide take the boat back while easing out the bow line until your stern is almost touching or even going past the rear post. Now you can make off the bow line to stop the boat going any further back and use one engine astern to bring the boat sideways towards the post, so your crew can thread the stern line through. The advantage of this is that you can see the crew and there is no danger of losing the bow on a gust of wind.

Once your bow and stern loops have been successfully attached, you can centre up the boat equidistant between the posts and relax.

If you're staying for an extended period you'll need to replace your looped lines with permanent lines to the rings. This is relatively simple now, as you can pull the boat fore and aft with the two looped lines to secure the permanent lines to the rings with a round turn and two half hitches, to prevent chafing, before bringing them back aboard to your cleats.

1 Locate the ring
In tidal areas, pile moorings have a ring like this one that slides up and down the riser bar with the boat on the tide. They usually have a thin line attached so you can pull them up and thread your line through, but locating them can be tricky.

2 Thread the bow line
It may be easier to put your first line around the riser bar then find the ring later. Threading the bow line from one forward cleat round the riser bar and back to the other forward cleat makes it easier to position the boat for the rear post.

3 Ease out the bow line
Once the line is looped back on board, direct the crew as to how much slack you want to allow the boat to reach the rear post. Make sure the line is made off before you engage astern to avoid hurting any fingers.

4 Thread the stern line

Once the bow line is made off with sufficient slack in it, reverse back to the rear pile and thread the stern line through. It's usually simpler to return the stern line to the same cleat rather than the one on the other side.

5 Using fenders If

your bathing platform doesn't allow easy access to the stern, consider rigging a pair of fenders horizontally, nose to tail, by threading each line through the other one's free eye before coming alongside the post.

6 Centre the boat With both

lines attached you can now centre up the boat equidistant between the two posts, either using the riser bars for a short stay or by re-rigging on to the rings for a longer stay to eliminate chafe.

INDEX

ADLARD COLES
Bloomsbury Publishing Plc
50 Bedford Square, London, WC1B 3DP, UK
29 Earlsfort Terrace, Dublin 2, Ireland

BLOOMSBURY, ADLARD COLES and the
Adlard Coles logo are trademarks of
Bloomsbury Publishing Plc

First published in Great Britain 2023
Copyright © Future Publishing Limited, 2023

A catalogue record for this book is available from
the British Library
Library of Congress Cataloguing-in-Publication
data has been applied for

ISBN: PB: 978-1-3994-1089-2;
ePub: 978-1-3994-1088-5; ePDF: 978-1-3994-1091-5

2 4 6 8 10 9 7 5 3 1

Typeset in Neue Haas Unica
Art Editor Louise Turpin
Printed and bound in India by Replika Press Pvt. Ltd.

MIX
Paper from
responsible sources
FSC® C016779

Photos and videos by Richard Langdon
To find out more about our authors and books
visit www.bloomsbury.com and sign up for our
newsletters